Online Side Hustle

Newbie-Friendly Guide for Making Your First $1,000 in Passive Income Each Month on Autopilot -- With 7 Proven Business Models Including Social Media, Shopify, and Amazon FBA

Written By

Financial Freedom Blueprint

Financial Freedom Blueprint

© Copyright 2019 - All rights reserved.

The content contained within this book may not be reproduced, duplicated or transmitted without direct written permission from the author or the publisher.

Under no circumstances will any blame or legal responsibility be held against the publisher, or author, for any damages, reparation, or monetary loss due to the information contained within this book. Either directly or indirectly.

Legal Notice:

This book is copyright protected. This book is only for personal use. You cannot amend, distribute, sell, use, quote or paraphrase any part, or the content within this book, without the consent of the author or publisher.

Disclaimer Notice:

Please note the information contained within this document is for educational and entertainment purposes only. All effort has been executed to present accurate, up to date, and reliable, complete information. No warranties of any kind are declared or implied. Readers acknowledge that the author is not engaging in the rendering of legal, financial, medical or professional advice. The content within this book has been derived from various sources. Please consult a licensed professional before attempting any techniques outlined in this book.

By reading this document, the reader agrees that under no circumstances is the author responsible for any losses, direct or indirect, which are incurred as a result of the use of information contained within this document, including, but not limited to, — errors, omissions, or inaccuracies.

Table Of Contents

Introduction   8

Online Marketing Mindset – what it really takes to succeed   9

Social Media Marketing   13

    Finding Your Niche   13

    Sponsorship and Collaborations   15

    Posting Videos   18

    Getting a Manager   20

    Existing Business Ads   21

    Working for Others   23

    Selling Your Own Products   24

    Pros and Cons   25

Shopify Dropshipping   29

    Dropshipping: The Business Model   29

    How to Get Started   31

    The Oberlo App   33

    Maintaining Your Shop   37

    Things to Remember   39

    Pros and Cons   43

Airbnb Agency   47

    Getting Clients   48

    Why Airbnb Agencies Are Important   50

    Think Outside the Box   54

    Coming Up With a Price   57

    Pros and Cons   59

Amazon FBA   64

    Benefits to Using FBA   67

    Fees and Pricing   69

    Helpful Programs   72

    Handmade Items   73

    Popular Items in 2019   75

    Pros and Cons   77

Kindle Publishing   81

    What to Write About   81

Financial Freedom Blueprint

    Is It "Book-Worthy?"   84

    Cover Appearance   86

    Submitting Your Work   88

    Spreading the Word   90

    When Will You Get Paid?   92

    Pros and Cons   93

Ecommerce Agency   98

    How to Select Which Business to Work With   98

    Getting Noticed   99

    How Much to Charge   101

    Know How to Operate the Business   103

    Get Them Customers   105

    Why Ecommerce is a Ridiculously Profitable   108

    Pros and Cons   110

Freelance Copywriting   114

    Negotiating Payments   117

    Getting Clients through Third-Party Websites   120

    Gaining Entrepreneur Skills   123

How to Build Your Reputation   124

Writing For Blogs   126

Pros and Cons   127

The Blueprint for Creating Success on the Side 132

Introduction

As technology pushes new boundaries on a daily basis, people are also becoming more savvy. 2019 is a year of growth, not only with internet-powered industries, but also with people who are seeking independence. Given all the different ways to make money online, both scams and legitimate sources, it can be difficult to know which route to take. This guide is meant to teach you about the most viable ways to make a side income, no gimmicks or pyramid schemes included! In order to succeed in these jobs, all you must provide is a few hours of time each week. There is no need to sell all of your stuff on Craigslist, or start a blog that will never gain traction. In a year where nearly anything is possible at the click of a button, it is time to learn how to make the most of your online presence, and turn your wisdom into an additional income.

Inside the book you'll find 7, proven business models which can have you earning your first $1,000/month online, faster than you could have ever imagined.

Online Marketing Mindset – what it really takes to succeed

The biggest thing that holds people back from making money online isn't a lack of technical skill or knowledge. Most "marketers" will give you the impression that there are a ton of secrets which you need to pay to know.

This isn't really the case. In fact, the biggest thing that holds people back is a lack of understanding about how money and competition works.

Most people have a scarcity mindset when it comes to money. There isn't enough of it, or that it's always running out.

This is what separates the rich from the poor, not intelligence or anything else. The rich have an abundance mindset regarding money, and the poor have a scarcity mindset.

"It's too late to make money online", or "other people are already doing it" are two phrases I hear regularly. These phrases imply there is a finite amount of demand and a finite amount of money in the world. Neither of these are true, and are prime examples of a scarcity mindset.

Ask yourself this, is there just one successful cell phone manufacturer? Absolutely not.

How many brands of beans do you see at the store? More than

one, right?

The fact is, there is more than enough demand in the world for anyone to be successful online. Particularly when we're talking about making your first $1,000.

And competition does not mean someone else has already "taken" all the money. Quite the contrary. Competition validates your idea, because people are already making money with it. Which means there is proven demand for what you're doing.

Thousands of people are making a good living (some even 7 or 8 figures a year) with the business models listed inside this book. And yet, there is still more than enough room for you, or anyone else, to come in an get your slice of the pie.

Let's break it down some more with math.

To make $1,000 a month, you need to sell

100 products @ $10

20 products @ 50

10 products @ $100

5 products @ $200

Now, if you have an online store (for example, I searched magnet car mounts, and the first site which came up was the below)

https://themagnetmount.com/

The "Wireless Charging Mount" on here is listed at $70. So the owners only have to sell 15 of these per month to make $1000.

That's one every two days.

When you consider there are 263 million car owners in the US alone. Do you think it'd be that hard to find 15 people willing to buy one? I don't think so.

Now, obviously there is more to it than this simple example, and I will expand on the technical details of each model as we move further on in the book, but I just want to illustrate just how easy it is to make money online in 2019.

So your lesson should be this, adopt an abundance mindset in everything you do. Do that, and the money will flow to you easier than it ever has before.

If you would like to hear more about the idea of abundance mindsets, then there are two main resources I would recommend.

The first is Robert Kiyosaki's classic *Rich Dad, Poor Dad*. You can pick up a copy on Amazon for less than $10.

The second is a lesser known work. *No BS Wealth Attraction in the New Economy* by esteemed marketing legend Dan Kennedy.

I prefer Kennedy's work as I think the practical examples Kiyosaki gives are somewhat dated, and in some cases, counter-productive to his theoretical advice. But both are worthy reads.

But for this book, we will focus more on the practical business models you can use to make your first $1,000 online.

Social Media Marketing

Did you know that thousands of people make money by simply posting on social media? This is one of the top ways to make a side income as a newbie, and you don't even have to leave your home! Essentially, social media marketing can be done anywhere and at any time. It does take a bit of skill and understanding, but once you have it down, it is a super easy way to see quick results. Because so many of us are already on these platforms, it only makes sense to turn it into something profitable; the audience already exists. Whether you like to utilize Facebook, Instagram, Twitter, Tumblr, or all of the above, there are existing opportunities for you to capitalize on.

Finding Your Niche

The work that must be done before you can start seeing results takes a bit of research -- you need to figure out what you are passionate about, and who is willing to listen. As mentioned, the audience is already out there, and it is your job as an influencer to pinpoint it. If you aren't sure which direction you'd like to take your social media accounts in, start by taking a look at the content that already exists. Consider the following factors:

- What kinds of accounts do you like to follow?

- Which of your followers has the most interaction?

- How frequently do your followers post?

This will give you an idea of what kind of accounts are already generating success. It can be a general rule of thumb that adding to a niche that is already thriving will allow you faster results. Your niche can be anything, really. There is an industry for those in the beauty field (hair/makeup/skincare/clothing). If you are into sports, you can utilize this by posting recaps and information about current events. Television shows and movies already have large followings; you can turn this into your own niche, creating an account that will focus on certain events involving the cast or posting reviews. Lifestyle is a huge niche that is currently trending in 2019 -- people like to see how others live, what they eat, and where they travel.

No matter what direction that you choose to go in, your niche will become your own personal brand. People respond well to accounts that are cohesive and consistent. If you start by making three posts a week, commit to this! Your followers are going to be expecting those posts, and if you stop posting for weeks at a time, this is when people will start to lose interest. Engagement is important, and aside from posting regularly, you also want to make sure that you are providing quality content. Think about it this way: Is this post something that you would like to see on your feed? Keep it interesting, and try to avoid filler.

Have an intention behind everything that you post. If you spam your followers with a bunch of filler, it is unlikely that they are going to want to interact with you. They might even become tired of the posts and decide to unfollow you. It is important to generate real engagement from real social media users. Once you have this platform built up, you would be surprised at who will take notice of your accounts. The more followers that you have, the more likely it will be for companies to want to work with you.

Because you probably already have these accounts in place, gaining more followers should not take much time out of your day. You can work on engaging with other users and posting quality content in as little as 5 minutes, right when you open your app. Engagement is anything from liking others' posts to leaving (or responding to) comments. Following similar accounts is also going to help you by building up a network of like-minded individuals.

Sponsorship and Collaborations

Once your follower count is up and you have active users that are interacting with your posts, the exciting part begins. Certain companies and organizations like to collaborate with social media users. Yes, that is correct -- these brands will pay you for simply posting on your social media accounts! It can be hard to determine a starting point at first; brands won't likely reach out to you until you are pretty established, but *you* can start reaching out to *them*. This will show initiative and drive. Paired with your consistent posts and follower engagement, your personal brand should be strong enough to participate in collaborations.

A good way to find these opportunities is to search for brands that are seeking "brand ambassadors." This is a term that describes a group of people who are chosen by a brand to represent it. This type of collaboration usually involves the company sending you their product (either for free or at a discounted rate), and then providing you with your own personal discount code that you can give to your followers. By posting content wearing/using/talking about said brand and offering a discount code, you are essentially generating new business for them.

Companies usually offer a type of commission-based payment rate, and the more sales that you generate for them, the more money that you will earn. As you can probably imagine, this type of collaboration can develop very quickly. Plus, the more that you do these collaborations, the more your engagement and follower statistics will grow.

Once companies see that your numbers are steadily increasing, they might even begin to send you their products for free. As long as they feel that your account and your personal brand is viable, they are still going to be benefiting from the exposure that you provide. Sometimes, brands will tell you a list of key points that they would like you to mention to your followers. When the details are included like this, a contract might also be a part of the deal. This is how sponsored post opportunities begin.

When a brand is sponsoring your post, they might provide you with some money up front (along with the product and a list of what they would like you to say to your followers). Of course, you need to use your common sense as the opportunities begin to arise. Stay true to yourself and your brand by only promoting companies that you actually support, and products that you actually have an interest in. Your followers will know that something is up if you begin promoting dog food on a makeup tutorial social media account, for example.

An alternative way to get noticed is by collaborating with someone who has a steadily rising profile. This can happen in several different ways. One way to get noticed is to tag larger accounts in your posts; make sure that what you are tagging this person in is relevant, because nobody likes spam. Having someone with a lot of followers repost something of yours is a great way to get noticed. Again, genuine interaction is best. Only tag others in content that is relevant and your own if you are trying to collaborate in this way.

As you build your reputation, you can try to message others to see if they would like to do an official collaboration. This can be something like each one making a post on the same topic/idea/theme and then mentioning the other person in the caption. This type of collaboration can be done with anyone; it is a great way to build your network and help out your fellow influencer. The same idea applies to brands as it does to other influencers: The more you collaborate, the more your reputation will grow.

Posting Videos

While a little bit more involved, creating your own videos is a great way to further connect with your followers and grow your brand. For example, if you are into skincare, making videos showing your various skincare routines will help boost your content rating. People like to see genuine content, so always try your best to be yourself in front of the camera. If you start making videos, YouTube is a great platform to grow on. Users on YouTube can utilize pre-placed ads to make money per click. By allowing YouTube to run these ads before/during your video, you will be making money each time a viewer responds to them.

The more you grow on YouTube, the more money you will be able to make. There is also a way to get paid per view on your video. If you notice that your view count is steadily rising, so can your income. There are plenty of resources available online regarding the various ways that you can make money by posting on YouTube. You don't need to have thousands of followers, either. As long as you are posting quality content, viewers will show an interest.

Your videos will become an extension of your social media portfolio. Brands like to see how you are in front of the camera, and might even offer you sponsorship/collaboration opportunities because of it. While posting videos isn't for everyone, if you are passionate about it, it can be worth a shot. Videos take more work than the average social media post. You will need to come up with a relevant idea, think about who your target audience is, and then record, edit, and post.

Once you get the hang of it, you might find that this brings you faster success than traditional social media posts. A common misconception is that you need a bunch of expensive equipment to get started with creating your own visual content. This isn't necessarily true. If you have a phone and a quiet place to film, then you are ready to get started. Think about what you would like to see in a video if you were the audience watching. No fancy gimmicks are needed to produce quality content.

If you are still unsure about getting started, do your own watching for a little while. Search for content that is similar to what you think you'd like to create, and take pointers from those videos. Think about the way that the YouTuber has outlined each video and how the background is set up. You'll probably a notice a pattern, because just the same as with other forms of social media, YouTube also follows certain trends that cater to what the audience wants to see. Notice the way that YouTubers title their videos and what kind of videos are popular in the moment. A lot of free information can be accessed, as long as you are willing to do some research.

Getting a Manager

When influencers gain traction in the industry, it is not uncommon to seek agency management. Getting an agent for your social media posts is the same concept as getting a talent agent. Normally, you must reach a certain level of followers/views before you are able to apply for representation. The rules are generally clear cut, so you should be able to visit the various agency websites to see if you meet the criteria for management. There are several different networks that manage users within the different industries. From makeup tutorials to comedy, you can obtain this representation to further your career in social media.

As mentioned, if you want to get one of these managers, you must be able to obtain a certain number of followers. The agency is going to want to make sure that it is representing an influencer that has what it takes to continue growing in the industry. This also involves signing a contract. Your manager will disclose what percentage is given to the agency vs. what you get paid. While some see this as a downside, others see it as an opportunity to have access to more jobs.

Your manager will apply for certain brand deals and sponsorships on your behalf. It takes a lot of the work out of approaching these companies for you. As long as you have a consistent brand to present, your manager will do the rest. This is how a lot of rising social media personalities take the next step. While you do not have to get representation to succeed in the industry, the option is there for you if you want to grow your brand even more.

Existing Business Ads

If you have an existing business that you would like to promote, you can do this by way of social media. The same rules apply to this type of an account as they do to a personal account. Your business is your brand, and you will want to make sure that you are staying true to your niche. Make sure that you are regularly engaging with your followers, and possibly even run promotions. Example: "Follow us on Instagram for a 15% discount!" You need to be just as savvy with your business account as you are with your own personal account.

A platform for you to run ads on your posts already exists within each app. Normally, you will make a post, and then you will have the option to "boost" or promote it. By doing this, your post will be pushed up higher into the algorithm. Facebook and Instagram have easily integrated ways for you to start doing this. By placing ads on other users news feeds that promote your business, you will generate more interest and potential new clients.

Payment for this type of advertising is usually on a pay-per-click basis. You begin by sorting out your parameters -- Who do you want to see this post? Selecting an age range and location gives you the opportunity to advertise to the exact demographic that you would like as future clients. Each time someone clicks on your ad, you are charged a small fee. When you are first creating your ad, you can select a maximum budget. For example, $20. The platform will take this budget and promote your post accordingly. This means the bigger budget you have to work with, the more the post will be promoted.

You don't have to shell out large amounts of money to advertise your business. Even for as little as a $1 budget, you can advertise. This is the benefit of using social media. You are self-sufficient, selecting exactly which users you would like to see your post. Also, you are not at the liberty of an advertising agency. Traditional business advertising usually involves a middleman and a much larger payment that is due up front.

Working for Others

If maintaining your own social media account does not interest you, getting a job where you represent someone else could be a nice solution. Plenty of people and businesses alike are trying to grow their brands; they are willing to hire others to help them grow. This is a perfect way to earn additional income, because it is usually not a full-time job. If you have a couple of hours to spend on social media each week, you will likely qualify. Finding a job like this could be as simple as offering to help a friend, or as official as searching job postings online. The level that you want to take it is up to you.

Some tasks that you can expect to be asked to do are: coming up with images/captions, making regular posts, liking others' posts, interacting with followers, and trying to get the brand noticed. Because of the way that this technology has developed over the last decade, many older businesses do not really know where to begin. This is where your skills can bridge the gap between old and new. A lot of business owners are grateful to find someone who is already knowledgeable about social media to help run their accounts.

Running social media accounts is also a great way to meet people in various businesses. Befriending your local business owners could come in handy for if you ever need their services or products in the future. A lot of what social media marketing involves is presenting a likable image to the public

-- This includes both the brand and yourself. It gives you the chance to be innovative, as well as creative. Many people enjoy this type of work as a side job because it allows the opportunity for more freedom than a traditional job.

A job like this could turn into something more permanent, if you choose. Beyond posting on social media, this type of job delves into the industry of advertising and the skills of being a personal assistant. Ask around -- you'd be surprised which of your friends, or even family members, would be willing to hire you in order to keep their social profiles current.

Selling Your Own Products

Have you ever come up with a business idea, but were unsure of where to begin? Consider social media! Plenty of people use their accounts to promote and sell handmade goods. This is a great platform to utilize for free advertisement. Another good thing about using social media to promote and sell your creations is that you do not need to rent a physical location to make sales. There are also many ways to accept payments via the internet through services such as PayPal, Stripe, and Google Wallet. With technology, so much is possible now that was never possible before.

If you aren't the type of person who enjoys making goods, you can use your social media accounts to promote different skills that you have. If a dancer chooses to post choreography videos on social media, this could lead to a growing personal brand and potential future job opportunities. The more that you are willing to put yourself out there, the better a chance there is of profiting off of your skills or crafts.

It can be intimidating to put yourself in front of a broad audience, but if you have a passion for something, it will show when you make posts and interact on social media. As long as you are staying true to yourself, others are going to take notice. The best part about doing your own advertising is that you get to control exactly how you'd like to portray yourself. It doesn't cost any money to make a few posts and gain notoriety. Over time, this just might be what your business needs in order to get a jump start.

Pros and Cons

Anyone can succeed in the business of social media marketing. All it takes is access to the internet and the willingness to interact with your followers. You need to be on top of current trends, and you must be tech-savvy. Growing a brand or advertising an existing one by way of social media is the perfect start to making a side income for the first time.

Pros:

- Work From Anywhere: You don't have to leave your home to make a post on social media. Interaction with your followers is fun and easy to do, and it can be done virtually anywhere you are. Because you don't have a rigid schedule to follow, social media marketing is even appropriate for those who already have a grueling full-time job. Whenever you have a few minutes to spare, you can get onto your accounts.

- Be Your Own Boss: The amount of work that you put into your social media marketing is up to your own discretion. If you want to go the extra mile and reach out to several brands daily, then you can. If you would rather grow your accounts organically and see what comes to you, you can also do that. The amount of time and effort you put into it is totally up to you.

- It Is an Ever-Growing Industry: Social media is a huge part of life in 2019. Almost everyone uses it, and it continues to grow rapidly. Becoming a part of something that is already thriving is a great business practice.

- There Is a Niche for Everything: No matter what you are interested in, there is likely already a niche that has been developed and a community of active users with an interest in it. Most of the guesswork has already been taken care of for you with social media marketing.

- You Will Enjoy It: Most jobs are stressful and fast-paced, but social media is something that you can do on your own time. It is likely that you already enjoy using social media daily, so why not turn it into something that can earn you an extra income?

Cons:

- You Need Patience: If you want to see instant growth, you will probably end up disappointed. While some people get lucky and get noticed right away, it is a rarity. It can take some time to build up your following and reputation, but as long as you are willing to put in the effort, you will start to see the growth.

- Be Aware of Scams: While a lot of brands out there truly do want your representation, some are looking to swindle you out of money. Be careful who you choose to work with, and just like any other business transaction, always read anything that they might ask you to sign. A simple observation of their profile is a good indication of a brand's validity. If you notice that their follower count is high, yet their interactions are computer-generated, steer clear.

- Luck is Involved: Hard work will get you places in any industry, but being an influencer does have an element of luck to it. You might be posting quality, consistent content, only to be overshadowed by someone else who is doing the same thing. This is why it is super important to solidify your niche and set yourself apart from the rest.

- Trends Change: Just as quickly as something rises to popularity on the internet, something else will come along and take its place. Because the web is ever-changing, you might notice that your followers will tire of your posts after some time. Be sure to leave room in your personal brand for transformation, just in case you see a decline in your niche.

- Beware of Fake Followers: Some people take advantage of the system by purchasing fake followers. While this does not earn them interaction, it boosts their numbers and makes them appear more appealing to work with. Companies cannot determine how or when you got your followers, but they do see the current number. This is an unfair advantage for those who work on getting followers organically.

Shopify Dropshipping

If you are unfamiliar with the company, Shopify is a platform that is designed to help you manage your own business. It is your one-stop shop for customization of an online portal for the products that you would like to sell. People use it for a variety of reasons, from selling clothing to art. It is cloud-based and easy for all to use. Many enjoy the perks that it comes with because the ability to list, manage, and sell inventory all in one place is highly efficient. Shopify gives you the opportunity to get noticed not only on social media, but on other online marketplaces and even physical shops as well.

Dropshipping: The Business Model

Because this guide is designed to teach you about ways you can make money online, focusing on Shopify dropshipping is going to be the smartest business tactic you can make. Operating your own business can take a lot of work, but with the dropshipping model, one of the most time-consuming steps is eliminated. Dropshipping follows a simple model -- the customer visits your ecommerce store and purchases a product at a retail price, you are paid a percentage of the wholesale price while paying the supplier the rest, and then the supplier sends the customer the goods directly.

Without having to worry about doing the shipping yourself, you will be free to further customize and streamline your ecommerce store. A lot of businesses, big and small, are turning to dropshipping for their business needs. If you are looking for a quick way to make extra money, this method can become very successful for you. Without having to be concerned with physically storing your inventory, you will have much more freedom than running your own traditional ecommerce store.

One of the most expensive parts of maintaining your own store is buying a surplus of inventory up front so that you have it in stock for your clients. This is where dropshipping can save you money -- You won't have to buy any inventory until you have officially made a sale. As you can see, even those with a very minimal budget can start an ecommerce store using the dropshipping business model.

Aside from not being responsible for inventory, you also don't have to worry about packing and shipping the products. This is a huge time saver for someone who is looking to use Shopify as a side income platform. Even if you already have a full-time job, or just have limited free time due to school, you can successfully run your own ecommerce business using the dropshipping business model.

Realistically, as long as you have steady internet access, you can run your business from your phone or laptop for less than $100 each month. As long as you are able to stay on top of communications with your clients and suppliers, you can even run your business on the go. With the help of your supplier, you won't have to worry about the business growing beyond your means. No matter how much it grows, as long as you are putting the orders in, they will take care of the rest.

Despite all of the convenience and flexibility, you must remember that this is still a business that you are responsible for. You will need to frequently check your emails and make sure that everything is running smoothly. While you are not alone in the endeavor, it is still your own business that you will be held accountable for.

How to Get Started

The first step is to create a Shopify account. This is your chance to create your username and business name. Even if you are unsure about what you would like to call your business, don't worry about it! You can change the name in the future. You could go from selling sports memorabilia to opening your own clothing boutique. The flexibility is an excellent feature. Creating an account is free for the first 14 days. They give everybody this free trial to see if owning an ecommerce business is the right fit for them. After this, a basic plan costs around $29 per month and can increase accordingly depending on if you would like to select a more advanced plan.

After your account has been created, Shopify will ask you

what brings you to the site. You can select options such as "I'm selling, just not online" or "I'm not selling products yet." Alternatively, you can even select "I'm just playing around," if you still are unsure about committing to running a business. Once you determine your reason for being on the site, then you will be redirected to your store dashboard. From here, you can control your listings and your themes. There is also a chance for you to set up your own custom domain.

The theme that comes with your store for free is the Shopify basic theme. There are plenty of other free themes that you can utilize. As you get more serious about your store, you can purchase a theme or hire someone to create a theme for you. Within each theme, you will be provided with customization options. This is where you can design your header and footer; you can also add photos to each section. Again, nothing is set in stone. If you design your theme to your liking, you can change it in the future when you think of new ideas.

Choosing your domain is a way you can help your customers remember your shop; it is a customized website name. If you select one on Shopify, your website URL will look something like this: www.xyz.myshopify.com -- While this isn't the worst format, it can seem a little bit long. But as a starting point, it is great and it is free. If you become more serious about your store, you can purchase a custom domain name that will change your website name to something a lot more simplified: www.xyz.com. Again, purchasing a domain isn't a requirement, but it could become helpful in the future.

The Oberlo App

Once you have all of the details of your account set up with Shopify, you will need to download an app called Oberlo. This app is designed by Shopify to work with their system. It is your place to connect with suppliers and to decide what kind of products that you would like to sell to your clients. Through a "Products" menu, you will be able to search through thousands of items. If you decide that you would like to sell several different products, this is possible through the Oberlo app.

Once you begin selecting products, you can link them straight to your Shopify store. The app also gives you suggestions and ideas for boosting your sales. They show you items that are normally sold together in stores, and allow you the option to add them into your own store. This can be the most time consuming, but most fun, part of the process. Deciding where you would like to take your brand is a very important part of operating an ecommerce store.

For example, a store that is called Picasso Plus might specialize in selling Picasso-themed items. This can include, pens, mugs, shirts, and more that display his artwork on each item. It might take some brainstorming for you to fully decide which direction you'd like to take with your store. Make sure that you are certain of your target audience, and then think about the kind of products that would be most appealing to that group. It is also wise to consider what you would find interesting. Think about what kind of products you would like to be included to buy online.

Using Oberlo not only provides you an organized way to stock your shop, but it also allows you the peace of mind to know that you are going to be working with verified suppliers. The app pre-screens each supplier to ensure that they meet the standards that are put in place by Shopify. Doing this on your own would pose too much of a risk, as you do not have the same tools at your disposal for the screening process.

Keep in mind that, during your supplier search, you will likely have to decide if you want your supplier to be located in the US or if you are okay with one that is based in China (or elsewhere). Including "ePacket" items means that you would like to give your clients the option to purchase these foreign-based products for low shipping costs. If you do not wish to do this, you can exclude this option when you are searching for products to stock your shop with. Naturally, US-based items are going to ship faster, but excluding ePacket items will narrow down your potential inventory options.

During your search for products, you can filter the results by price points. If you have a specific vision for your shop, you can determine the minimum or maximum amount that you would like to sell an item for. When you are performing these product searches, you will be given a rating for each item. This will help you to decide if you'd like to list said item in your own store. Oberlo has plenty of resources to assist you as you build your store.

Stocking your shop is as simple as clicking a button. As mentioned, the products that you select on Oberlo get linked directly to your Shopify account. Keep in mind the following as you are stocking your store:

- Make sure that you are writing accurate product descriptions. Oberlo provides you with the basic details that you need, but modifying each one is a way to make the connection that you have with your clients more personal.

- Choose what you think is a fair price. Oberlo sets a default price for you, but you have the option to modify this. Do some research on your own, and see what other sellers are offering for the same or similar products. Your shop won't succeed if you are selling an item that appears very overpriced in relation to other shops.

- Because the shipping time is not up to you, disclose to

your customers what their estimated wait time is. It is best to be very transparent about this in order to keep your customers happy.

- In the beginning, it is recommended that you select about 10-20 products to start with. This will give your store enough variety, but will also keep it looking organized and maintained. As you see how your clients respond to the given items, you can then modify your stock. You can either swap or add items as you see fit. This is the best way to run your shop when you are just starting out on Shopify. By doing this, you won't be wasting time on writing a ton of product descriptions for products that might not even be desired by your client base.

It is all a matter of trial and error when it comes to running your own business. While it can be hard to just wait and see, this is what normally needs to be done. Oberlo will show you what your statistics are, and from there, you will be able to see which items are most in demand. When you do decide to expand your inventory, try going based on the trends that you see, either in your statistics, or in other shops that are similar.

Once you have your list of products linked over to your Shopify account, you can go in and create different categories or "collections" for the items. This will be a way for you to organize everything and make sure that your clients have an efficient shopping experience. With this, you just have to use your common sense to determine which items should be placed together. This is another great opportunity to imagine yourself in your clients' shoes. What would you expect to see in terms of categorization?

Maintaining Your Shop

Much like a shop with a physical location, you are going to want to monitor customer activity as your business develops. Remember that Oberlo will be able to give you some insight into this. If you notice that your customers are responding well to mugs in the first month, consider expanding your selection. The Shopify App Store is a place where you can search for additional places to source your products. The following are some examples:

- POD Shippers: POD stands for print-on-demand. A POD shipper will allow you access to a range of fully customizable products. This is where you can let your creative side flourish -- designing the looks of your products via these third party apps will give your shop a unique edge.

- Specialty Shippers: This type of shipper is normally meant for products that you cannot get in your home country. Some people use specialty shippers to sell their clients goods, such as coffee. This can be a cool element to introduce to your Shopify customers.

- Aggregate Shippers: For larger quantities of items, some that are even name brand items, you are going to want to look into an aggregate shipper. Sometimes, if your shop gains traction quickly, it is smart to switch over to one of these larger shipping companies.

Aside from making sure that your shop is fully prepared to handle its orders, you are also going to need to do some customer outreach. Being more personable toward your clients will make them feel valued. There are a couple of different ways to make sure that you are communicating effectively with your clients. The first way is by creating and utilizing social media pages for your business. Not only does this give you multiple platforms to advertise on, but it also gives your clients a way to easily contact you and give you feedback on your shop.

Another way to stay in touch with clients is by having them sign up for marketing emails that you create. Shopify has ways to do this that are already built in and ready to be accessed by each shop owner. Remember, this about the content that you would like to receive from a retail store. There is no need to spam your clients with information that is too repetitive or not relevant. Stay short and concise -- a lot of successful shops offer discount coupons within their newsletters in order to entice customers to join the mailing list.

Consider your use of SEO keywords. Even in your short product descriptions, you should be thinking about the way that you are utilizing certain keywords. If your shop is SEO formatted, you will be appearing higher in the search engine results. If you are unsure of how to format your shop with the correct keywords, you can take a look at some of Shopify's built-in tools that are designed to help.

Things to Remember

The role of the dropshipper is an invisible one. The customer sees your store as the interface, and goes off of what they see there to determine if they would like to make a purchase. You are the direct link between your customers and the products that they receive, even if you are not the one who is doing the packing and shipping. This is why communication is so essential as a shop owner. For any order-related inquiries, your customers are going to be counting on you to keep them in the loop.

You are also responsible for relaying any messages from the shipper to the customer. If you know that the shipper is located in China and requires a 2-3 week ship time, then it would be morally incorrect to tell your customers that they can expect their products in 1 week. Simple business practices like this one will set you apart from being a scam type of shop to a successful one that customers can trust. Word of mouth can be a great free source of advertisement. If you make a good impression on one person, they might go ahead and tell five of their friends.

Presentation of your products matters, too. If a customer were to click onto your shop, and all of the items were disorganized and hard to find, it is unlikely that they are going to make a purchase. You have to remember, much like any other traditional business, you have competition. If a customer does not find your shop streamlined and appealing, there are plenty of other places on Shopify (and elsewhere online) where they can spend their money. The more effort you put into your presentation, the more it will be recognized.

When you first start out on Shopify, you will probably have to make a checklist to ensure that you are doing everything correctly. Hold onto this list, and keep referring back to it as your shop develops. Even if you are not just starting from scratch, some of the information could be a valuable reminder to yourself. Owning your own business does require a lot of hard work and effort. Just because you do not have to physically show up to a workplace does not mean that it will automatically be a breeze. You will need to wear many different hats and utilize several of your skills, from designing the theme of your shop to providing excellent customer service.

Some of the items on your checklist can include the following:

- Get Your Domain Secured: Even if you start out with one of the domain options that are available through Shopify, you will probably need to think of some domain name ideas for the future. Having your own customized domain gives your shop a professional look, and it makes it easier for your customers to remember your shop.

- Secure Your Payment Portal: In order to get paid for your sales, you will need to make sure that your customers' payments are going to go through. The easiest way to do this is by making a test sale using your own card information. Once you make sure that everything works, you can refund yourself so that no money is lost.

- Make Sure Landing Pages Are Completed: When you launch your shop, you should make sure that all pages that your customers have access to are finished. This involves everything from selecting a theme, writing content, and adding images. Aside from a standard home page, some other popular landing pages are "About" and "Contact." Both are important for different reasons -- The "About" page explains your shop mission, while the "Contact" page lets customers know how they can get in touch with you.

- Review Your Email Settings: Through Shopify, you have access to several email templates that send out automatically. This is a great tool to utilize, because it makes client outreach effortless. You can go into these templates and create your own edits, making sure that you are sending the right message to your clients.

- Audit Your Content: Running your own store can be a lot of work, so it is wise to get an outside opinion. Have a friend or family member view your store, and allow them to provide honest input. This is also a great time for catching small spelling errors or possible broken links.

- Streamline the Images You Choose: If your site loads its images at different speeds, this could be because they are different sizes. Try to resize your images to the same or similar size. This not only promotes cohesiveness, but it also lends a more streamlined look to your shop. Also, try to select images that go well together. This could mean anything from having a similar theme to having the same color scheme. Your shop will appear more professional if the images make sense together.

- Install Analytics: While Shopify provides you with their own sets of analytics tools, it might be wise to also set up a third-party tool to keep track of your site visitors. You will be able to see where your customers come from, what time they visit, and how long they spend on each page. This information can come in handy when you are trying to decide how to market your products.

Pros and Cons

Utilizing Shopify for dropshipping is becoming increasingly popular. Because of the wide variety of products that can be kept in stock, many people find it is a great way to quickly start up a business. The tools that Shopify has to offer truly makes the process simple and accessible for all, no complicated software included.

Pros:

- You Can Sell Nearly Anything: No matter what kind of shop you open, you have a wide array of products to choose from. Whether you want to specialize in customized mugs, or if you want to stock an entire clothing store, Shopify gives you the platform to grow on.
- Your Shop Can Be Broad or Niche: The freedom to customize your shop at any time is great for your own

personal branding. Whether you want to create a specialty shop, or one that appeals to the masses, anything is possible.

- No Physical Commitment: You are never required to be anywhere at any given time. This is what makes Shopify dropshipping a great option for making quick money online. The products essentially sell themselves, and you only need to monitor this in the background. There are no in-person meetings or interactions to worry about.

- It Can Be Easily Expanded: If your shop shows a promising amount of growth, keeping it stocked up is as easy as pressing a button. Since you do not need to worry about purchasing huge amounts of your inventory in bulk, you will easily be able to accommodate your customers if they begin to multiply.

- It Pays for Itself: Once your Shopify free trial is up, you must pay a monthly fee to keep your shop running. The business will very easily begin to pay for itself within the first few sales that you make. This type of turnaround in a business is very rare, but the Shopify platform makes it almost effortless.

Cons:

- It Is an Investment: Yes, owning a store on Shopify costs money. With that membership, though, you are a platform with plenty of different tools that will help you out along the way. If you are not prepared for this monthly commitment, then owning your own business is probably not the best step for you to take in order to make additional income. You might also have to deal with a slight overlap in getting paid and ordering the customer's product. It is wise to prepare for any type of possibility.

- You Might Not Gain Traction Quickly: While there is a chance to greatly succeed on Shopify, it is important to remember the risk involved -- you are going to have to rely on a bit of luck. Building up your reputation with your customers can take time, so remember that as you are first starting out. Your success probably won't happen overnight, but if you stay committed to working on your shop, you should start seeing tangible results.

- There is Competition: There is a high chance that you will have direct competition on Shopify. This is okay! Use this as motivation to do better. Think about all of the different places that you can choose to buy a mug. What are some of the factors that help you narrow down where you would like to buy a mug from?

Thinking about things from the customer's perspective will help you a lot when it comes to the way that you operate your shop.

- You Aren't in Control: When you sell a product to a customer, you are then relying on your shipper to do the rest. This can be both a relief and a burden, at times. Because it is out of your hands, you need to be prepared to take the brunt of the situation when shipping takes longer than expected or when a customer has a missing item in their package. Steady communication between yourself, your customers, and your shipper is essential for running a successful business.

- Expect Low Profits to Start: Your business will need to grow gradually, so you can expect your profits to the do the same. You are getting a percentage of the profits when you decide to partner with a drop shipper. Many people are discouraged by this, but you will likely be thankful in the future when your shop is bigger and you do not have to worry about packing and shipping.

Airbnb Agency

Airbnb has become a huge industry in several cities all around the world. It is often a cheaper and better way to explore a city that you are visiting, all without the need to stay in a single hotel room for the duration of your trip. Being a part of an Airbnb agency does not involve renting out your own living space. Instead, you are helping others rent out *their* homes. An Airbnb agency is designed to help the property owner and the renter connect. Sometimes, these agencies even offer services such as setting optimal pricing for the home, restocking items in the home, and cleaning the home. Of course, if you are looking to make an online side income, you would only need to be a part of the services that would suit your own schedule.

You can start your own agency, and you can even have others working for you, all from the comfort of your own home. In order to manage an Airbnb agency, you need to have excellent communication skills; this is going to make or break the business. While you do not physically need to meet with renters, you will want to make sure that you can stay on top of your emails and notifications. The main role of an Airbnb agency is to bridge the gap between the property owner and the renter. In case anyone needs help or has questions, you must be available to assist.

As you can imagine, you will need to have an extensive understanding of Airbnb and the process of renting. This is not very hard to learn, especially if you have ever rented a space on Airbnb yourself. There are several tutorials and videos online that go into all of the details that you will need; it just takes a little bit of well-thought-out research. Once you are knowledgeable enough on the industry, you will need to make a decision: Do you want to team up with an existing Airbnb agency or do you want to start your own?

Depending on how much time and money you have to start with, it might be easier to go with an existing agency in the beginning so that you can get a feel for the business. Either way, you are going to want to make sure that the agency explains its services very clearly. Some strictly offer booking/listing services, and you are going to want to make sure that your customers understand what you have to offer.

Getting Clients

In order to get Airbnb owners to work with you, the way you present yourself is very important. Like it has been mentioned, having personal experience with Airbnb (either as a renter or an owner) is a big plus. Your clients are going to trust you more if they trust that you have an understanding of the industry. Gaining this trust is essential, because without property owners that are willing to work with you, there would be no need for an Airbnb agency. The trick is to convince the owner that they would be better off using your services than listing their property on their own.

Explain the services that are being offered in a clear and concise way. You will not want to imply that the agency will clean the home and provide key exchanges, when the only services offered are booking/listing and vice versa. Credibility is everything when it comes to this type of business. You should not have to offer your clients any gimmicks in order for them to be willing to work with you; it should be very black and white when it comes to what you have to offer. Once you have secured the client base, the business should flourish naturally.

Essentially, these properties are being put into your hands, so you must prove to your clients that you are able to deliver your promise. Tell them why they should work with you, and be honest about what you have to offer. This is the best way to succeed in an industry involving home rentals. A good approach is to mention that other property management companies can be too big and overpriced. Many consist of several different employees and ask for too much of a percentage of the profit. Being a part of a smaller agency will allow the customer to talk to the same person (or few people) each time. This personal connection builds trust in an easy way. Simply knowing who they can turn to with questions and concerns will give you a higher chance of gaining their business.

Why Airbnb Agencies Are Important

One of the main reasons a person might want to use an Airbnb agency is to avoid being scammed. Unfortunately, there are many people (property owners and renters alike) who do try to scam others for money. Renting an Airbnb through an agency is a way to ensure that you are making a smart, pre-screened selection. Also, a lot of property owners are merely renters themselves. This means that someone who is renting an apartment might be listing their apartment on Airbnb for a brief time while they are elsewhere. This isn't always a scam, because some landlords are okay with subletting. But, it can be illegal, and a lease violation in some places. If you are renting someone's apartment without landlord permission, you might be in for an ugly surprise if the landlord finds out.

Another reason a property owner might want to seek out an agency to work with is because they simply don't want to deal with the follow-up that comes with Airbnb. If the property owner is also on the go, it might be inconvenient for them to have to keep up with communications from potential renters. It can often be an overwhelming process, so taking on the help of a third party to bridge this gap makes sense.

It is the intention of an Airbnb agency to make sure that

everything that is going on is safe and legal. Both the property owner and renter will be thankful to have that middleman to monitor such activities. In order to do this, you must be efficient with time and organization. Attention to detail is a must. You won't want to accidentally double-book a property or forget to pay a client. While being a part of an Airbnb agency is a more involved way to make money online, it can become a very successful side business for you to rely on.

From the start, you should have a system in place that you can follow. These standard procedures should cover your bases, and can be referenced along the way in case you encounter any issues. For example, there should be a plan in place both before you begin operating and during your operations. Some things to consider are the following:

- Think about whether you would like to join an existing agency, or start your own. Both are realistic ways for you to make money on the side, but naturally, starting your own Airbnb agency is likely going to be more time consuming because of the extra steps that you will need to take.

- Decide which services you will provide. As mentioned, some Airbnb agencies are full service. They start by booking/listing Airbnbs, and they continue to assist with everything from the key exchange to the restocking of the home. No matter how extensive you would like to get, just make sure that you know what you are getting yourself into from the start.

- Make sure that you are all caught up on the basic rules and regulations that surround the Airbnb industry. Knowledge is everything when it comes to being a part of a successful business. You need to be able to confidently answer any questions that come your way.

- Once you are ready to start working, come up with a basic outline of what you need to do each day in order to keep the agency running smoothly. This can be anything from answering emails, to ensuring that all listings are properly uploaded.

- Decide on your niche. Sometimes, it can be helpful to differentiate yourself from other businesses; this will give you less competition. Instead of only listing regular apartments/homes through your agency, maybe you could only focus on properties that are beachfront. This is a way that you can set yourself apart from the crowd. Anything can become your niche, and some brainstorming might be required.

- Consider how you are going to handle payment exchanges. You are going to need a valid and safe system in place if you want to get paid. Selecting a payment portal will also take a certain amount of research on your end, but there are a wide variety to choose from available online.

- Become familiar with the properties. When your clients come to you with their properties that they would like you to list, take the time to actually look into what they have to offer. How many bedrooms are available? Is it a shared space, or is it a private space? It will show your dedication if you are able to provide a detailed listing versus some generic write-up of your clients' properties. Remember, you are trying to make these properties as appealing as you can to the potential renters.

- Don't be afraid to hustle! A big component of an Airbnb agency is getting your client a decent price on their listing, and this can involve some negotiation. If you know that your client is expecting an unreasonable amount of money for their rental, you need to be able to provide them with valid alternative suggestions. Be diplomatic, yet honest, and explain how you came to your conclusions on price points. This can take a little bit of practice on your end, and becoming familiar with other listings on Airbnb is a great way to get this experience. Look for listings that have similar features, or are in similar areas. This is the best way to choose a smart, yet fair, price point.

Think Outside the Box

Remember that there are several different ways to run the same business. If you would like to start your own Airbnb agency, you can specialize in different niches, as it was mentioned before. Plenty of people like to stay by the beach when they are on vacation. If you live in an area that has access to water, using the beach as a niche is a quick way to gain traction and appeal. It is an automatic selling point, and it will keep many different people interested in the properties that you have to offer. If you are located in an area with forests, you can try to seek clients that are looking to rent out their cabins to others. Renting a cabin in the woods is a classic vacation that plenty of people take, and it might even be more feasible for people to rent an Airbnb instead of going through expensive cabin rental agencies.

Another niche that you can use is large spaces. Often, people will decide to rent an Airbnb over a hotel room because they have a lot of people that would like to all stay together. This is possible in an Airbnb, especially in larger homes. If you have plenty of space to offer your clients, this will solve the need for renting multiple different units. You might also get recurring customers, because they will know that you have the rentals that can accommodate all of the people in their party. Alternatively, people rent out their small apartments on Airbnb, and someone who is traveling alone might see this as the best option. Instead of paying for a hotel room with all of the amenities included, spending half that price on an Airbnb apartment might make more sense.

Airbnbs that are pet-friendly can also become a niche for you to utilize. Not every hotel or motel accepts pets, and if they do, it is often for a sizeable additional fee each night. Some people who rent out their homes are perfectly okay with guests bringing along their furry friends. Use this to your advantage, and make it a selling point. A lot of people like to travel with their pets, so they are going to need special accommodations. The great part about Airbnb is that you will find a wide variety of spaces that are available for rent, so using pet-friendly locations as a niche can become something that you are well known for.

Once you are settled on a niche, you can use other perks to your advantage. Express to your clients that, by using an Airbnb agency, they are going to be able to spend more time enjoying the vacation and less time worrying about the planning. You will need to allow them to see that you are there to help, and that your service is meant to make the planning easier. The same goes for the property owners: You need to show them that using an Airbnb agency is more helpful than trying to list their own properties.

In order to accomplish this, you must have great people skills. No matter if you choose to run your own agency, or become a part of an existing one, you will be communicating with people frequently. This job can definitely be a side hustle in addition to a regular full-time job, but the more effort you put into it, the more success you will begin to see. As long as you are able to spend a little bit of time on it each day, then you should have no problem keeping up with your clients' needs.

People are going to want your opinion on different marketing strategies. This is another main reason why someone would want to list their property via an agency. Expressing your opinions and providing advice is also going to become a part of your daily task list. You don't need to have a degree in marketing, but you do need to make sure that you are up-to-speed on the current most successful marketing techniques in order to help your clients. It is okay to think outside of the box; be honest with your clients, and bounce some ideas off of them to determine what would be the best way to list their properties.

You can mention the different niches that you have thought of, and various other selling points. Basically, anything that adds value to the property, whether it is merely for looks or serves a greater purpose, can be used as a positive selling point. See what your client has to say about the space, and you will probably think of even more ways that you can market the property.

Pro tip: Advertising properties as "the only" gives them an extra air of exclusivity, and thus, allows you to charge higher prices.

E.g. "The only 3 bedroom beachfront property on this street", "The only Georgian townhouse on the Upper East side with an elevator for wheelchair users." You might not think a particular property is unique, but if you think outside the box, you'll be sure to come up with something.

Coming Up With a Price

Arguably the most difficult job when working with real estate, you must come up with a fair price point to list each Airbnb. Not only do you have to set a price that is fair to the property owner, but you must also set one that will appeal to the potential renters. It might be difficult to simply take a look at a property and then decide on a number on the spot. You can use a few of these techniques for determining your price points:

- Get an idea of what other similar properties are being rented for. You wouldn't want to list a 2-bedroom home for $200 a night when similar homes were being rented for only $100. To compare these figures, you might just need to get on Airbnb and do a little bit of filtered searching on your own.

- Once you have seen what similar properties are being rented for, do a broader search of the city or town. It is unlikely that someone is going to come into town and rent the only expensive property while the rest remain in a lower price bracket. It takes a simple search and some common sense to ensure that you are within the means of the price bracket.

- Have a conversation with your client before the listing goes up. In addition to what you would like to say about the property when you list it, you will be discussing the pricing with your client. Whenever you present them with numbers, make sure that you have credible reasoning for why you have chosen them. Example: "I think that you should rent your home for $80 a night, because similar homes in the areas are seeing success at this price point." It is all about incentive when you are trying to make a sale.

- Don't forget the time of year that the client is trying to rent out their property. If it is a holiday season, it might be more valid to charge a little bit more money for the rental because of the higher demand. You wouldn't necessarily want to list a place for the same amount in June as you would during Christmas. Take a look at the calendar on Airbnb when you are doing your comparative searches.

- If your client is new to renting, it would be worthwhile to suggest that they try to keep their pricing down in order to be competitive. Without an established reputation in place, having a lower price is a major selling point. Especially because the AirBNB platform relies so heavily on user ratings. As renters begin to give the property ratings, this will boost its popularity and place it in higher demand. After this, you might be able to suggest raising the price.

Pros and Cons

Working in an industry that deals with accommodation is a sure way to stay relevant. When travel is involved, visitors are going to need a place to stay. Working as an Airbnb agent also provides you with the chance to help people. Not only is it an important job, but it can also become meaningful. You will get to interact with a variety of people and learn about various properties.

Pros:

- It Can Become a Lucrative Career: Doing work in real estate always has the potential for growth. You might find that you enjoy it enough to take things to the next level. While being a part of an Airbnb agency can start out as an online side hustle, it can just as easily transform into your full-time business.

- The Industry Will Always Be in Demand: People are always going to need places to stay when they travel.

Unlike other industries, you will always find a market for those seeking vacation rentals. This is a great factor in deciding whether or not you would like to become a part of the industry. No matter when you join, there will always be plenty of demand.

- You Will Learn a Lot About Your Area: By listing various properties all over your city, you might discover new places that you have never seen before. This can come in handy for when you would like to rent your own vacation home, or even if you are looking to move your permanent residence. By default, you will be more familiar with the area that you reside in, because you are often going to be comparing similar properties.

- You Get to Help People: By connecting renters to property owners, you are bridging a gap and allowing the business transaction to operate smoothly. If you enjoy working directly with people, you will likely find interest in working for an Airbnb agency. This can be a nice change of pace if your day job does not involve much outside interaction. You will have the ability to let your personality shine through and to get to know others.

- Use of Creativity is Encouraged: Appeal is what you are striving for when you are listing properties for rent.

Your client is going to be counting on you to get them the best rate for their rental. Alternatively, renters are going to be searching for the best place to stay during their vacations. This is when you can allow your creativity to flourish. You will be able to use photos, descriptive keywords, and niches in order to convince renters why they should choose the given property as their rental. You can have a lot of fun with this part, coming up with ways that you think might appeal to the masses.

Cons:

- It Can Become Time Consuming: While being a part of an Airbnb agency qualifies as a side hustle, it might become a lot to handle for a single person. If you are already working a full-time job and you are trying to list properties during a busy holiday season, you might find yourself overwhelmed with the amount of work that you are responsible for.

- It Is a Commitment: Because you are not putting your own property up for rent, you do not get to just decide that you don't want to put in the work any longer when you get tired of it. The property owner will be counting on you to fulfill a commitment, so you probably don't want to get on board with a job like this if you are not in it for the long haul. You need to make sure that every aspect of the rental goes smoothly, from the listing to the check out.

- Seasons Impact Growth: As previously touched upon, the need for a vacation rental during a holiday season is much higher than during any other average time. While there is always a fairly steady stream of demand, you might not see the most growth during the seasons that are not peak seasons. If you are looking for fast money, you might want to consider working in the industry during some of the most high-demand times (Christmas, Thanksgiving, New Year's Eve, etc...).

- Conflict Can Arise: When you are working with any number of people, it can be easy to clash. You will need to make sure that the rental process goes smoothly for the property owner and the renter, so if you are not up for the role of mediator, then you might want to reconsider working for an Airbnb agency.

- You Might Get in Over Your Head: If you are just starting out in the industry, it might feel a bit overwhelming. In order to prevent any unnecessary stress, you should start out with an Airbnb agency that is already well established. Having a team of people to help you out with your workload will likely be better than trying to take on all of the tasks by yourself from the start. After you have the experience under your belt, you will likely be more successful if you decide that you want to start your own agency.

Amazon FBA

FBA stands for "Fulfillment By Amazon," and it is becoming a fast-growing way for you to make extra money. This service is very similar to a dropshipping service; you are able to sell a wide variety of products through your own store on Amazon. Once you have your inventory scheduled, you will then send it off to an Amazon warehouse in bulk, and then they will take care of the rest. Once sales are made, the warehouse will ship the items to each individual client. This streamlined way of running a store is the best way to operate your own business when you are looking to make some extra income on the side.

The Amazon Marketplace is an ecommerce marketplace owned by Amazon that will host your store. Because of this, you will have exposure to anyone who chooses to browse Amazon for products. As you can imagine, the amount of people that shop on Amazon each day is exponentially growing. One difference between a regular dropshipper and this one is that you can sell products that are both new and used. If you have some items that you are no longer using, you can list them on your store to earn some quick money. It's like a virtual garage sale. There is a real opportunity for success if you decide that you'd like to sell products by using Amazon FBA.

How to Get Started

The first step to selling on Amazon is to make a Selling on Amazon account. From there, you can then add FBA as one of the features on your account. These first few steps are simple and should only take you a couple of minutes to complete. Before you begin, you might need to consider what you'd like your business email address to be, because you should sign up for your account with that designated email. If you are only going to be selling a couple of your own items and you do not wish to create a business email, then your personal one will work just fine.

Once your account is set up, you can begin listing your inventory. You can start to add products to your catalogue one at a time or in bulk. If you are experienced and have inventory management software in place already, you should be able to just upload your existing inventory directly onto Amazon. The same thought process goes into FBA as it would with any other dropshipping business. You will need to figure out what you would like to sell.

Start by considering if you would like to stock your shop with items that are already listed in the catalogue, or if you would like to sell your own items. Depending on which direction you decide to go in, your next action can vary. If you are selling your own used items, you will need to take a little bit of extra time coming up with the proper photos and descriptions for each one. If you are going to be selling handmade goods, this will also require extra time for obvious reasons.

The easiest way to begin on FBA when you are looking to make quick money is to stock your shop with products that are already listed on Amazon. This method does not require any additional work on your end to gather/supply the products. If you need shipping supplies, Amazon has you covered. You are able to buy product prep supplies directly from the source, and they have plenty of Amazon-preferred packaging to help you easily get your items to their warehouse.

There are several tools to assist you during this process. Amazon partners with carriers that offer discounted shipping rates. This way, you will be able to keep your inventory stocked without breaking the bank. These discounts are available if you are looking to ship small/individual parcels or items that are shipped on pallets (either less than a truckload or an entire truckload). With these parameters, you will likely qualify for the discounts that are available.

Aside from the discounted rate, these partner carriers also supply things such as shipping labels. All you will need to do is order all of your items, pack them up, and place the predetermined label on the box. Keep in mind that if you are going to be shipping truckloads of items, you will need to have a dock and forklift. This type of service is for shops that are bigger and well-established. When you are first starting out, you will likely only be sending a few boxes at a time to the warehouse.

Benefits to Using FBA

Once everything is fully stocked, you will be ready to make some sales. This is when you will see the return on your investments. A great thing about partnering with Amazon is that your customers will receive the same customer service that any traditional Amazon customer would. The interface looks exactly the same, and any questions that arise will be sent over to Amazon to be dealt with. This takes a lot of pressure off of you as a seller, because you don't have to be the one to answer to your customers' inquiries or concerns. As you can see, this is another way that FBA differs from traditional dropshipping systems.

For anyone trying to make a side income online, it is important that the business provides as much convenience as possible. With FBA, these needs will be met. You do not have to worry about physically storing any of the inventory at your home. All you must be responsible for is the ordering and bulk shipping to the warehouse. They provide your items with a space to stay until a sale is made. With this type of system, it is possible for anyone to open a successful ecommerce store. A lot of people are seeing fast results that generate additional income.

Because your shop is being "hosted" by Amazon, your products will pop up on their search results. There are millions of searches daily for just about anything that you can think of. Amazon does their best to boost the product listings of those being sold by FBA users. This means, if someone is looking to buy bandages, Amazon will try to boost your search result over a larger name-brand company. It is a way to receive built-in advertisement that is provided to you because you have decided to partner with Amazon.

Your item can also qualify for Prime shipping, Amazon's expedited shipping service. This is a huge perk to those customers who are looking to get their items quickly. As long as they have a Prime membership in place, they will be able to select Prime shipping on any of the items that you are selling. This is another form of built-in advertisement. A lot of times, customers put on search filters to only show Prime-ready items.

Because Amazon has been around for such a long time, and is a well-established business already, you can have the confidence to know that your customers will be taken care of. Even if you are brand new to ecommerce, you are covered under an umbrella that has a team of people ready to help you and your customers. This is a much easier way for you to start a shop rather than attempting to sell your items organically. The Amazon platform already exists, and the opportunity is as big as you would like to make it.

Fees and Pricing

Using FBA is an investment, so if you are unwilling to put money into your business, then this is not the right business for you. The bottom line is that you will need to be willing to stock your shop with inventory before you can begin seeing a return profit. You will also need to consider the cost of shipping to the fulfillment warehouse. If you are unsure about this business model, you can start by shipping one single box of items to the warehouse for your inventory. When this runs out, then you can decide if you would like to continue running your own store.

With FBA, it can cost anywhere from $2-$5 to ship items to the warehouse. If you have oversized items, the price can be anywhere between $8-$150. There are shipping rates on Amazon that you can refer to when you are deciding what size box you will need to send. Even if you decide to send the smallest box of inventory to the warehouse, your customers will still have the same access -- they will be able to purchase products from your store, speak with customer service, and process refunds if need be.

There is a small storage fee that is required if you have inventory in the Amazon warehouse. The fee is deducted monthly, and it depends on the month of the year and the amount of average space that your items are taking up. Between January to September, the fee is $0.69 per cubic foot for a standard storage unit and $0.48 for an oversized unit. For October-December the pricing is $2.40/$1.20. This pricing goes up due to holiday demand, but keep in mind that you will likely also see an increase in sales during this time.

Amazon does provide you with a small price cut, as you can see, if you decide that you need an oversized storage unit. By selecting this unit, this means that you are likely more serious about your shop and plan to keep it regularly stocked with items. If you are still unsure about which plan that you will need to get started, opt for a standard unit. You can always change this in the future if you need more space.

If you are still on the fence about FBA, you can go online to use their price calculator. Not only will you be able to estimate your out of pocket fees, but you will also be able to see what your estimated profit will be. There are also a couple of product example charts for you to get an idea of how much space certain items require while in storage. For example, to store a 1-pound box of T-shirts, the average cost is around $3.68 per unit.

There is a special program in place called FBA Small and Light. This is for shops who know that they are not going to have a large amount of inventory, and it is great for first-timers who are still becoming familiar with the process. This service will help you by offering reduced fulfillment costs to certain items that can be ordered in smaller quantities. By keeping the costs down, your profit margins will naturally go up. This can be an excellent starting point for a beginner.

Another great thing is that there is no minimum purchase requirement when it comes to the Small and Light program. Your customers will receive the same great perks and service that they normally would. They still qualify for free shipping, and if they are Prime members, they will also qualify for the expedited Prime shipping option. If you think that this sounds like a good option to start with, take a look at the catalogue for qualified items.

An additional way that you can help your customers save money is by opting into Amazon's Subscribe and Save program. With the products that qualify, customers can agree to purchase your Subscribe and Save item, which will result in recurring deliveries of that item. It is a chance for your customers to conveniently get the items that they need, as well as you having a regular customer and sale. By obtaining customers through this program, it is also likely that they will return to your store and make more purchases.

Even despite your small investment, Amazon makes it easy for you to obtain business and keep it. They want you to succeed, because it is a mutually beneficial partnership. This is why using FBA will likely generate the success that you expect, instead of trying to open a store using only your own resources. Anyone can operate a FBA store, and any item(s) can be sold. The freedom to turn your store into exactly what you want is there, and the only thing you need is consistent initiative.

Helpful Programs

You should already be familiar with the different programs that Amazon has to offer, but here are some that you probably have never considered:

Permission to Sell Dangerous Goods -- It's good to have a niche, and in this case, you can have one that allows you to sell items that are normally not permitted to be sold via ecommerce websites. Through Amazon FBA, you are able to join a waitlist to get approval on selling these "dangerous" items. Some of which include: perfumes, household cleaners, paint, and certain beauty products. These items are in demand, but often hard to a first-time seller to obtain the rights to sell. Amazon gives you this opportunity if you wish to take it.

Sponsored Products -- Much like traditional social media marketing, you can also utilize sponsored posts to promote your items. There is a pay-per-click service available that allows you to put ads on Amazon. You only pay for the ad each time that it is clicked on, and you can set a maximum budget for your campaign. This is a great way to get noticed on the Amazon Marketplace.

Lightning Deals -- Amazon offers certain items at a discounted rate as a part of their Lightning Deals program. This is a limited sale of a certain item, and its exclusivity entices customer to make immediate purchases. If you would like to participate, you can set some of your items to be available as a deal in order to give your business a boost in sales.

Global Access -- You aren't limited to your local area when it comes to sales. If you wanted to, you could take your shop to the next level and sell globally. Obviously, this is quite the expansion of your client base. There are many different global programs that you can become a part of, from worldwide selling to targeted regions.

Handmade Items

The process for selling your own items is similar to selling pre-selected inventory. Of course, you will have to consider that the supply and demand levels are going to be much higher when you are creating the items that are for sale. If your shop becomes popular in a short amount of time, you will likely need to work extra to create enough inventory. Amazon has a community with creators from over 80 countries that sell their own handmade creations. If you would like to become a part of this niche, the application process is easy. Amazon still helps you with fulfillment, and you would send your creations to the warehouse the same way you would with any other inventory that you choose.

Amazon likes to screen all new applicants to ensure the quality of the items for sale. They don't want to mistakenly allow a seller a spot in the homemade marketplace when their items are actually just being purchased and resold. That is what the standard Amazon Marketplace is for. Once you meet the approval criteria, you are given several tools to utilize in your homemade shop. Just like any other shop, you have the opportunity to customize it to your liking. You can create a unique URL so that your customers will remember your shop easily.

Listing your handmade goods costs nothing. Everything from the process of joining Amazon Handmade to creating your shop is free. When you make a sale, Amazon will keep a 15% referral fee, and that is the only catch! It is a worthwhile business move, especially if you truly do not have much to invest. When making your budget, all you will have to think about is the time and money that you are going to spend creating your products. Remember that these figures can increase by a lot if your shop gains traction.

If you aren't the most crafty person, you can still sell on Handmade if you like to customize ready-made items! For example, if you are good with a paint brush, you can paint custom mugs for people. Getting a large stock of basic mugs and some paint and brushes likely won't cost very much money, and it will be perfect to get you started. Your creativity can be unlimited on Amazon Handmade.

As was mentioned before, the same features of traditional Amazon FBA apply -- Once an order is placed, Amazon will pack and ship the item to your customer. All you have to do is keep your inventory stocked at the Amazon warehouse. This can turn into a very lucrative side business that allows you the freedom of running your own businesses and the creativity to make custom products for your client base.

There are plenty of success stories that you can read about on the Handmade homepage. You might even be able to gather some ideas for your own shop. The best part about opting for this type of program is that there are less shops for you to compete with. One-of-a-kind items are often items that customers are willing to pay more money for, so you could find a lot of success in a very short amount of time if you choose the right niche. Take a look at what some of the most successful shops on Handmade are selling; it's the best way to see what kind of items are in demand.

Popular Items in 2019

If you truly don't know where to start, the following are some popular niches that sellers tend to find success with:

Drone Accessories -- Drones are a very high-demand product nowadays, and because they are becoming more and more affordable, a wider variety of people are purchasing them. They are customizable in many ways, so if you stock a shop that has various different accessories, you will likely find some recurring customers.

Posture Correctors -- Everything from seat cushions to neck pillows, posture correctors tend to do very well on Amazon. Because it is so convenient to order these items online, without the customer having to go to a specialty shop, you will likely find it easy to gain clients if you have some of these types of products in your shop.

Phone Cases -- Nearly every single person has a cell phone these days, and most like to keep them protected. Phone cases are relatively inexpensive, and in very high demand. You are almost guaranteed to make a sale if you keep some phone cases in stock.

Pro tip: Don't just go with stock plastic and rubber cases. Funky cases like bamboo, graphite and carbon fiber are all the rage, and you can charge premium prices for them.

LED Lighting -- Customizable lighting features are very trendy right now, and there are products that can appeal to a wide variety of people. This is another fairly inexpensive item that you can keep your shop stocked with. From light bulbs to strip lighting, this is a niche that features plenty of unique finds.

Pros and Cons

It is no secret that Amazon is a huge platform that has continued success all over the world. When you are looking to make an extra income, it makes sense to join a team that is already thriving. With Amazon FBA, you will get a taste of what it is like to run your own business. You also have the option to let your creative side run wild, if you choose.

Pros:

- It Is a Convenient Way to Sell: If you are going to select a platform to sell your items, why not go with one that is already ultra successful? Amazon has already made a name for themselves, so you don't have to work as hard to convince customers that your platform is a reputable one. Your customers will also get all of the traditional perks that other Amazon customers receive. Everything from the packing, shipping, and customer service -- Amazon will take care of it all.

- The Search Algorithm Helps You Advertise: Without even asking for advertisement, Amazon's algorithm takes action. FBA sellers automatically get priority in the search results. This allows you to be seen by more people and gives you the opportunity to gain recurring customers. One of the hardest parts about starting your own business is informing people about it, and Amazon takes care of this for you automatically.

- **Prime Shipping Applies to Your Products:** Anyone with a Prime membership will be able to receive your items with Prime shipping. This means that they will get their items faster and with no additional charge. This is just another way that Amazon works in your favor, keeping customer satisfaction up from the very beginning.

- **You Can Sell Virtually Anything You Want:** With Amazon FBA, you have an unlimited opportunity to sell any product of your choosing. You can stock your store with items that can commonly be ordered in bulk, you can have the opportunity to sell "dangerous" goods like perfume and beauty supplies, you can sell used items that you no longer have a use for, or you can even create your own items. The ball really is in your court when it comes to the selection that you can put into your inventory.

- **The Amount of Time You Devote Can Vary:** If you just want to put a few items into your store and never stock it again, that would be fine. Or, you can grow your store into a larger entity that always has bulk items in stock. The frequency in which you stock your store is truly up to your own discretion. This type of an online job gives you the flexibility that is essential when you have other things going on in your life. You don't necessarily have to prioritize your store unless you want to.

Cons:

- Costs Can Get High: Having your own Amazon store is a pretty big responsibility. You will need to pay for your account/inventory storage, so keep that in mind before you decide whether opening a store is right for you. Most of the time, people see a return in their investment, but it can take some time. The important thing to remember if you want to stick with it is to be as patient as you can.

- You Must Ship Items to the Warehouse: When you are sending your items to the inventory warehouse, they must be packaged correctly or else Amazon will not accept them. Make sure that you clearly understand all of the guidelines that are in place before you take the time to make a shipment. If you do this part incorrectly, you might have to pay additional fees for Amazon to fix the packaging.

- Delays Can Happen During the Holidays: Amazon is a

huge hub when it comes to online gift shopping. During the busiest months of the year, especially around the winter holidays, items that you keep in stock might become unavailable or delayed. If you cannot gain access to these items, you will have to wait until you can restock your own shop. This can be frustrating, especially if you want to participate in the holiday rush.

- You Can't Make Your Own Email List: After you make a sale, you do not have the right to your customer's email address. This isn't necessarily a negative thing, but if you wanted to send out mass emails to existing clients, you wouldn't be able to do so. A lot of business owners like to have this information in order to promote special deals to their existing customers.

- Branding is Out of Your Hands: If you have a vision for your shop that involves a logo, you won't get you use it on your boxes. Unfortunately, using Amazon FBA means that all of your customers will receive standard Amazon packaging in the mail. This isn't a big deal to some, but other business owners might see a certain vision for their company that won't be possible to pursue via FBA.

Kindle Publishing

If you have something to say, why not share it with the world? Kindle Publishing gives a voice to those who write. It is a self-serving platform that writers can utilize in order to publish and sell their work. Once you have some content to work with, you can edit this on Kindle Publishing. With their various tools, you are able to customize your writing to your liking. There is even a chance to create your own book cover if you do not already have one that you are working with. After this, you can decide if you'd like to publish in ebook format or in paperback. Kindle will help you with all of the finer details of publishing. When your book has been published, it will become available for sale on Amazon This platform makes it possible for just about anyone to publish their own work.

While publishing a book can sound like an overwhelming task, it is one that you can easily achieve. This is an excellent way to make a side income, because the book will continue to make you money after you put in all of the work. With Kindle Publishing, you will have plenty of resources and references to use during your writing process. They make publishing as easy as possible; you will be able to focus more on spreading the word about your book than the technicalities involved with creating your content.

What to Write About

Even if you don't consider yourself an "author," there are likely plenty of topics that you are able to write about. Think about what genuinely interests you -- Do you have any passions? What are you knowledgeable about? Would you like to help people? This part can often be the hardest; in a way, it is the process of choosing a niche for your book. When you publish something, you are creating your own personal brand. You need to consider how you would like to present yourself to the audience.

Are you going to come from a self-help writer point of view? Would you like to create a work of fiction? The possibilities are endless, and this period of self-discovery can be very fun. Take as much time as you can to brainstorm all of the different ideas you can write about. Also, write often! Even if you are just writing in a journal, these thoughts can turn into some tangible ideas. You need to be able to be honest with yourself and your own thoughts, as this transparency will allow you to access your best ideas.

Once you have a few topics, set aside some time each week to free-write on these topics. Staying inspired during the writing process can be difficult. Aside from not knowing what to say, you might also find yourself distracted. Ensure that you are giving yourself a fair chance to sit in peace for an hour or so. Unplugging from screens and other electronic devices can be super challenging, especially when they have become such a huge part of our society. The writing process can become very similar to a meditation. Just allow yourself to process your thoughts and ideas, writing them down as you go along. Remember, there is no right or wrong here -- just express yourself!

After you have some content to work with, you can start to refine it. Create a new document and consider it your rough draft. Examine your writing and try to decide if what you are saying is what you would like to convey to the audience. This process can vary for everyone, but using an organized method like this will help you to decide what you'd like to publish. At this point, getting outside opinions can be helpful. If you feel comfortable, bounce some ideas off of family members or friends. You can even join some social media writers' groups to share your work. Getting honest feedback will further refine your content, so be open to what others have to say.

This process is going to take time, and the amount is unknown. Unless you want to set a deadline for yourself, you do not need to stress out over the time it takes to write your content. Some people do it over a year, others can do it in weeks. Keeping a tentative timeline can be handy; this will also provide you with the motivation to push through any writer's block you might experience. The bottom line is that you should always want to make the process enjoyable. If you aren't enjoying what you are doing, then you might need to reevaluate the steps that you are taking.

Is It "Book-Worthy?"

The process of writing a book can often bring up some feelings of self-doubt. You might ask yourself -- "Will anyone even care about this if I publish it?" This feeling is 100% normal! Think about all of the different niches that there are. Thinking about any topic and you will be able to do an Amazon search and find a book on it. If you are worried about your audience not being receptive to your work, the focus should actually be on who you are marketing to rather than what you are marketing. Try your best to boost your morale as often as you can. Remind yourself that publishing your own work is a huge accomplishment and that your hard work will pay off. This can be hard to realize when you are still in the developmental stage of pre-publishing.

Having a support system can be great to alleviate any doubts that might come up. Even if you aren't sharing your work with others, you can tell those closest to what you are up to. Talk about your goals and why you are working hard to publish your work. This support will boost you whenever you are feeling down, and it will help you whenever you have those moments when you feel like giving up. These feelings are bound to come up, so don't stress over them too much.

On a more statistical note, if you are worried about sales, then you can spend a little bit more time doing research before you begin your rough draft. Take a look at the current literary trends. What kind of books are on the bestseller lists right now? Do any of these topics appeal to you? Talk to your friends, too! What kinds of books do they enjoy reading? Anything that is being purchased frequently can be considered a current "trending topic." While these topics can change often, it might help you decide on which direction that you'd like to take your writing.

For another entirely different approach, you can write about something unique that isn't trending. If you have something that you'd like to write about that isn't currently on the charts, go for it! Adding a niche to a market can be a risk, but it might pay off because there aren't many others like it in the same category. Remember, you get to determine what is "book-worthy," not the audience. Even if you do not see a lot of immediate sales, you can work extra hard to market your content to the right people.

Whether you are an experienced writer or you are new to the field, these self-doubting tendencies can creep up at any point in time. By knowing how to boost your confidence in a healthy way, you will be able to overcome these feelings and continue with your publishing process. Talking with others who are in the same boat can also be essential to overcoming any worries you have. As was mentioned, there are many existing groups online that revolve around the writing and publishing process. Becoming a part of one gives you the chance to vent and bounce ideas off of like-minded people.

Not a writer? No problem.

There are many ghostwriting companies who will write your book for you after you submit an outline. This obviously costs more, but saves you a ton of time and effort.

Prices start from $1.50/100 words, so a 12,000 word non-fiction book will set you back around $180.

Popular companies include

http://theurbanwriters.com and http://ewritersolutions.com

Cover Appearance

As you are making progress with writing your content, you should also be thinking about branding. What do you want your book cover to look like? This part can seem overwhelming to beginners, but you have plenty of options thanks to Kindle Publishing:

Hire Someone -- You can hire someone to create your book cover. Even if you have no idea where to begin, hiring an artist or graphic designer to create the cover for you is a great first step. After you decide on someone that you would like to work with, you will likely have a consultation that will allow you to come up with some ideas. Do you want your cover to be cohesive with your title? Do you have a different vision?

Draw It -- If you consider yourself a capable artist, you can create your own cover! Taking your art and turning into a digital image is one way for you to create your own cover art. You will be able to upload it onto Kindle Publishing and customize the font using the Cover Creator tool after that.

Use the Tools -- Something in between drawing the cover art yourself and utilizing help from others is using digital images and then customizing the cover on Kindle. You can take art that has already been created (with permission) and then use it to build your book cover. The great thing about Kindle is that they give you these tools for free.

This part is creative and fun! It allows you to decide what visual image you would like to use to represent your written work. If you start thinking about this while you are still writing, this will give you plenty of time to bring it into fruition before it is time to publish. Remember, this part can be changed or customized. If you finish writing and then you realize that your cover doesn't truly represent the work or doesn't fit the niche, you can change it.

For an ebook, creating the cover is simple and does not

require much editing. You will decide what you would like it to look like and what it should say. The measurements aren't as big of a deal since the content is going to be visual. When you are deciding on a cover for a physical paperback book, you will need to make sure that your cover art fits the Kindle guidelines. Luckily, Kindle will not allow you to publish anything that doesn't meet the requirements. They will assist you with any resizing that needs to be done. You will also have options to decide on paper color and finish.

Even if you have no experience with creating a book cover, Kindle makes it easy for those of all skill levels. If you have any specific questions, there is also a great guide that has been complied with several FAQs that have been asked (and answered) by other writers. You should be able to do this all yourself with the help of these resources. Alternatively, if you are using a graphic designer to design the cover, you can talk about the sizing with them ahead of time to make sure that everything is going to meet the guidelines.

Submitting Your Work

Once you have your content and cover ready for publishing, Kindle will guide you through the final steps. Uploading all of your work is as simple as the click of a button. If anything must be changed before the final publishing, Kindle will inform you of what that is. Their system is intended to be very transparent, so you are as prepared as you can be. When you upload your manuscript, it should already be it its final form, fully edited. The Kindle system will do a light scan of it to further ensure that there are no additional errors.

The same process will happen with your cover art. Depending on if you are releasing an ebook or a paperback, Kindle will update you accordingly with what must be done in order to meet all of the standard requirements. As mentioned, uploading the cover art for an ebook is easier due to the fact that it remains digital. A paperback will be distributed physically, so the quality must be higher in order to ensure that your book is going to look as professional as possible.

Once all of your work has been uploaded, you get to fill in basic fields such as title and description. These fields are what will be displayed on your Amazon product page, so make sure that you are accurately representing your work in a detailed fashion. Kindle then gives you the option to select certain categories for your work, for example: Fiction, Non-Fiction, Poetry, History, etc…The options are endless, so try your best to select the 3 that best represent your writing.

Pricing is further explained during this stage of publication. Kindle offers two different royalty programs. There are benefits that can be explained in greater detail, but they offer plans that provide you either 35% or 70% of the money to you as the author; Kindle keeps a percentage, too. There are certain qualifiers that must be met to qualify for the 70%

royalty program, so do some research before you make your final selection.

Once all of these details are chosen, you will submit everything to Kindle and then wait for the approval. Normally, approval is decided pretty quickly (24-72 hours). If anything must be changed, you will receive an email with these requests. Once you receive your approval, it can take up to 72 more hours for your book to appear in the Amazon store. This is an exciting moment for all writers; it takes all of that hard work that you have put in and turns it into something tangible that you can be proud of.

Spreading the Word

Once your title is available on the Amazon Marketplace, you can feel free to talk about it on every platform that you are a part of. Make posts about it on social media, tell friends and family, and do anything else that you see fit in order to get the word out. Remember that being proud about something you worked hard on is nothing to feel embarrassed about; you must generate some noise in order to get the sales started. Users can organically come across your title on Amazon, but doing your own independent marketing will bring you even more success.

If you want to give your book an even bigger publicity boost, you can pay for some basic advertising. Nearly any app has the option now to utilize pay-per-click advertising. Whether you choose to do this directly on Amazon, or from your social media accounts, you can compile a post that will target certain audiences. Doing this will create even more buzz about your title. Each additional person that buys your book is another opportunity for word-of-mouth advertising. This is exactly how it sounds -- When someone buys your book and talks about it with other people, this is "word of mouth."

Giveaways are a great tactic to use when you are releasing something new. Offering a copy of your work for free can generate curiosity about the book. Amazon provides you with ways to set up your own giveaway. You get to pick the algorithm and the amount of winners, a fully customizable experience. This tool is always available to you as a writer on Amazon. If you feel that you ever need to re-generate the buzz about your work, try doing a giveaway! This will also feature your product on the Amazon Giveaways homepage, yet another way for your work to get noticed by people who are browsing.

Getting ratings on Amazon is a free way that you can boost your sales. Verified ratings of your work will help others to determine if they would like to give it a read or not. Encourage your customers to leave a rating and a review once they have read your work. This is a great thing that you can ask of your friends and family members who are likely willing to vouch for you. Books with higher ratings do better on the Amazon charts and are boosted on the algorithms. Try your best to obtain as many ratings as possible from your readers.

You need to be strategic with your advertising plan. Of course, you want your book to be successful with a lot of sales, but don't get caught up in spending too much money on advertising. If you are purchasing ads every week, you might end up spending more than you are making. Another thing to keep in mind that you are not going to get paid by Kindle instantly. That part takes time, so factoring this into your budget is essential if you are just starting out as a self-published writer.

When Will You Get Paid?

As you begin your journey as a writer on Kindle/Amazon, you will have to provide your bank account information, or an alternative way to get paid. Direct deposit to your bank account is the easiest way for you to get your money quickly. You will also need to fill out your tax information, because being a self-published writer involves paying takes, just like any other standard job. You can expect to see your first paycheck 60 days after the end of your first month's sales. This is the payment schedule that Amazon follows for royalty payments.

Imaginably, doing this for a side income does involve a lot of patience and effort, but you can just as easily become very successful. This type of job will pay for itself over time, and as long as your book stays on the market with sales, you can expect to see a continual paycheck. This is why marketing is essential after you release written work. You need to keep your audience engaged with and excited about your book in order to keep generating sales. This part can require some creativity on your end. Think about ways that you can advertise that would naturally catch your own eye.

A big component to being successful as a self-published writer is luck. It does take luck to get noticed sometimes. No matter how hard you work, selling a book requires you to have a willing audience. If you find that certain marketing approaching aren't really generating many sales, you can try different ones. The whole process will likely be a bit of trial and error until you can determine what works the best. Once you get into the flow of marketing and selling, you will see your royalties flowing in without a problem.

Pros and Cons

If being an author has ever seemed out of reach, Kindle Direct is here to prove you wrong. With all of the tools that you will need for self-publishing, you can work with Kindle to turn your ideas into a literary reality. This process can be both exciting and practical – Many people find that their books sell themselves.

Pros:

- You Will Be A Part of the Largest Ebook Market: Through the Kindle/Amazon marketplace, several authors find success when publishing their written work. Because the market is so large, there is a niche for just about anything. This means that you will likely find success, as long as you are able to find the right marketing techniques.

- You Can Sell Worldwide: Because Amazon is accessible by people all around the globe, your book can be, too. Without ever having to leave your computer, you are able to make sales in several different countries. This instant-access type of market is great, especially if you are just starting out in the industry.

- The System is Simple: Even if you have never published written work before, the step-by-step process makes it easy for you to do everything that you need. The need to hire an outside source isn't necessary unless you choose to. From editing to creating cover art, you can do it all on the Kindle Publishing website.

- Amazon Has Built-In Marketing Tools: From ads to giveaways, there are plenty of chances for you to promote your product. You can easily set your marketing up from your Amazon author page, and it will give your content the boost that it deserves. The best part is, there are no additional fees to use these services.

- Get Your Money Directly to Your Bank Account: Direct deposit is an option that you can choose for your royalty payments. Just like any traditional job, you can report and receive your income the same way. This is a lucrative job that is well-respected and will serve you well if you put in the effort.

- Leverage the ever-growing audiobook market. Amazon owns Audible, and thus, after you get your book narrated, you can upload it onto there as well. If you have a book in a popular niche, then it's not uncommon to make $1,000 a month on Audible alone.

Cons:

- It Takes Time to Get Paid: Not only do you need to make sure that you are making sales, but when you do make them, it takes up to 60 days for you to see that profit. Unfortunately, this is just the system that Amazon has in place for sending you royalty payments. If you are looking for instant gratification, then self-publishing likely isn't going to be right for you.

- Writing Takes a Lot of Preparation: Writing a book is a big deal! You are going to need to put in a lot of prep work before you are able to enjoy any of the benefits. This involves: coming up with a concept, writing drafts, editing the final outcome, putting together the publishing details, and more. If this is something that you truly enjoy doing, then writing a book should not be a problem for you. As long as it is enjoyable, you should have the motivation to keep pushing forward.

- Marketing Can Be Difficult: Talking about your book is something that you might need to practice, but it is necessary if you want to make sales. You will need to choose how you would like to represent yourself, and make social media posts that reflect this. Advertising on your own this way is one of the most common sources for self-published authors. For one, it is free, so you won't have to worry about spending more than you make. You just need to be willing to put in the time to think about creative ways to get the word out about your book.

- You Will Have a Lot of Competition: While your book will be for sale on the biggest digital marketplace in the world, that also means that you will have a lot of direct competition. It can be hard to get noticed when there are so many other writers out there that are self-publishing and using Kindle/Amazon as a platform.

- You'll Need to Keep Momentum Going: There is a lot of buzz that surrounds a newly released book. Once this energy dies down, it is up to you to keep customers interested in buying your work. This part can be a bit discouraging at times, and you need to develop the determination necessary to not give up when you are no longer seeing sales.

Ecommerce Agency

Ecommerce is a topic that should already be familiar to you -- Instead of stocking and selling products online, you can actually work in ecommerce as an assistant to businesses that are already up and running. An ecommerce agent's job is to boost sales for ecommerce shops. Every online business must market their products in order to make sales, and it can be your job to help with this process. In a couple of simple steps, you can get online businesses to pay you for helping them grow in the marketplace.

How to Select Which Business to Work With

As a consumer, you should already have a basic idea of the kinds of stores that exist online. You probably purchase items online on a regular basis. Before you begin your job as an ecommerce agent, you should consider which types of businesses are in demand. Remember, the selection process works both ways -- the business will survey you just as much as you survey it. A good starting point is to determine if said business has a product that people will actually want to buy. While finding a specialty clock store online might be unique, it likely won't be as successful as a modern watch store. You just need to use your common sense to figure out if spending the time to work with a business is going to be beneficial.

This is a chance for you to really zone in on what you are

interested in; do some research in some of the industries that appeal to you. Just about anything and everything can be purchased online, so it shouldn't be hard to find some stores that appeal to you. As you are narrowing down your options, keep in mind how realistic the products being sold are. Is there going to be a use for them now? A few years down the road? You will want to consider the future. Selecting a dying industry can be a huge mistake and will put an end to your side income.

Once you have your eyes set on a couple of businesses, take a look at the way they represent themselves online. This is essential in the field of ecommerce. Make sure that they have a website that is updated and functional. Also, take a look at their social media presence. A business that already cares about both of these aspects is going to be a lot easier to represent and promote. While it is going to be your job to make sure that they keep up with their online marketing activity, you shouldn't have to put in 100% of the work.

Getting Noticed

Once you have some potential clients to work with, one of the most important steps comes next -- You have to bridge the gap. The following are some strategies that you can utilize to approach these businesses:

- Draft an email: Before you make contact with a

company, you should determine what you are going to say. You'll want your approach to be the right amount of professional, but also friendly. Of course, if you are working for an ecommerce agency, the agency itself should also be able to guide you through this process.

- Eliminate any spam dialogue: When you are about to send your initial email, read over it to make sure that none of it sounds like spam. Think about if you were to get the email as a business owner -- Would you read it or delete it? If the content does not sound natural, you might want to rethink your approach. Remember, your initial email should be a conversation starter rather than a sales pitch.

- Be transparent: In your email, you will want to explain exactly what services that you will provide to the business. There should be no guesswork done by the owner. Talk about how you can help the business grow and what tactics you will use to get it to that point.

- Discuss pricing: Some find it taboo to talk about pricing right away, but bringing it up from the start can save you a lot of time. If a business owner does not agree with your price point, it is better to know right away than wasting your time going back and forth with negotiations. Set your price and stand firmly where you set it. You need to have confidence in the services that you provide and the amount that you deserve to be paid. If you are working with an ecommerce agency, there will usually be predetermined prices that you must charge.

- Point out their flaws: This is not meant to insult the business, but if you notice that the website could use improvement, include that detail in your pitch. Acknowledging the existing marketing that a business has in place not only shows that you are actively thinking about how you can make it better, but it also shows your involvement from the start. Taking a few minutes to look at a business's online presence will allow you to sound more professional as you initiate contact and provide recommendations. This gives the business owner an idea of the what the future holds by working with you. Being able to imagine real results is a great push for why that business should hire you.

How Much to Charge

If you are starting your own ecommerce agency, one of the hardest things to decide is what to charge for your services. Especially when you are just starting out, it can be difficult for you to put a value on what you can do for other businesses. It is recommended that agencies start with a minimum of $1,000 per month for each business that they help. This might be well above the amount that you were originally thinking, but it is a well-justified starting figure. A big mistake that is often made by ecommerce agencies is charging too little for their services.

When your prices are too low, customers might begin to take advantage of you. They might become needy or demanding, and the work will eventually outweigh the profit. You will want to make sure that you are paid comfortably for all the services provided. The odds are that 1 out of every 10 clients will say yes. You will have to get used to the idea that there will be rejection. Some might even point out that your pricing is too high, but if you know your worth, you will be able to stand firm and continue to the next prospect.

There are some exceptions: If you are working with a business that wants to recommend a friend who becomes another client, giving the original business a discount would be a nice sort of referral system. You would be gaining more clientele, so it would still be considered a gain for you. This type of mindset is important when you are entering the ecommerce industry. You need to be strategic and detailed, always one step ahead of the game.

Another incentive for standing firm with your price point is the fact that this is a side job for you. While you probably already have a main source of income, you won't have to rely on this money in order to live. Having an additional income means having an extra source of money that should essentially be easy to obtain. If you find yourself putting in more work than what your money's worth is, you might want to reconsider whether you are charging enough.

Know How to Operate the Business

Much like any other job, you will have to do some training in order to succeed. Whether you begin working for an existing agency or you decide to start your own, having basic ecommerce knowledge is essential for the future of your success. The secret to being good at your job is knowing how to do all of the various tasks that come with it. You will need to know how to set up an ecommerce shop. The easiest way to do this will be by utilizing a platform, such as Shopify. If you need practice, set up your own test shop so that you are familiar with the steps.

If you are able to walk a business owner through something, your skills will be considered more valid. By placing a business on Shopify, you are helping them branch out. Assuming they do not already have a Shopify account in place, you can begin by setting one up for your client. With your knowledge about the platform, it can be your job to set up, maintain, and monitor this online shop. Because Shopify is so easy to use, it is frequently going to be a great starting point when you are working with ecommerce.

Having basic knowledge about web design is also going to

strengthen your skills as an ecommerce agent. This can be learned by doing some reading and by creating and editing your own websites. Remember, you are going to be aiming to work with ecommerce businesses that already have decent websites in place, but you might need to perform a little bit of maintenance from time to time. You will always want to stress how important having a functional website is. Potential customers see a business website as a portal for how the owner runs the company.

If a website is hard to navigate, the business will likely lose clients due simply to lack of organization. It is your job as an agent to streamline this. Even if the website itself has decent content and updated HTML, you might need to suggest a little bit of clean-up work. Think about what you can do for the website in order to make the browsing experience as pleasant as possible. Making sure that the customers can see all of the products offered and easily make a purchase is going to be one of the main components of your job.

Encourage your clients to aim for innovative marketing strategies. People like to see visual representation when they shop. Are there enough photos on the website and with the product listings? Is there a chance for the customer to see a video that corresponds with the products? Small steps like this can make a huge difference in customer engagement. Your aim is to grab the attention of these customers to turn the intrigue into sales. Think about what would impress you if you were browsing on the website. What would make the client select the given business to make their purchase?

There is a fine line between creating a spark and coming off as a gimmick, so be wary when you are making suggestions to your client. You will want to be interesting enough to draw attention to the shop, but not be perceived over the top. This type of balance can often take practice, but you will quickly learn what works and what does not work in your given industry. Being in the ecommerce field does take a little trial and error.

Never make promises to your client that you cannot keep. Telling a client that their business is going to grow by 500% in a month is not realistic. Make sure to keep up with the transparency, even after you are hired. It is your job to work together with the business to form strategies that will draw in business. If something isn't working as well as you planned, go back to the drawing board and try again. You will want to encourage the business owner to try new things, because sometimes, people will overlook the same old marketing strategies.

Get Them Customers

Helping a business grow means you are essentially going to help them make sales. This becomes possible by gaining clients, and that is where your help comes in. An ecommerce agent makes it a point to effectively market the business in order to gain the attention of the customers. You need to effectively convince customers why they are making the right choice, and this can be done by using a few different methods:

- SEO Keywords: Make sure that the business website is SEO-formatted. What this means is that whenever a potential customer makes a search online using designated keywords, the business will come up near the top of the search results. By doing this, you are allowing the consumer to make a quick selection. Nobody likes to search for hours when they are in need of something simple. Being near the top of the search will likely earn that business customers by way of convenience. You can get higher rankings in search engines by adding the keywords customers are most likely to use when searching for your products to the ecommerce site's web copy.

- Hold a Sale: Listing a product for sale might increase the likelihood of visitors finding the ecommerce shop. Everyone likes getting discounted items, and while they are browsing, they might even find other products that they would be willing to buy. Having a sale every so often keeps the business engagement up.

- Put a Code on Social Media: This tactic kills two birds

with one stone -- Provide a discount code on social media that customers can use on the website. This will not only encourage people to follow the social media pages, but it will also attract visitors to the website. Again, people love to save money whenever possible. Giving out a discount code to a select audience promotes a sense of exclusivity.

- Start a Blog: Companies that have blogs on their websites allow customers to see the more personal side of the business. A blog is a great way for the business owner to introduce their staff and give potential customers an inside look as to how the business operates. Adding a blog to the website will not cost the business any money, and it will be an additional source for advertisement and promotion. It is a great way to connect with customers with no added hassle. SEO keywords can also be utilized in blogs, so keep that in mind when they are being written.

- Make the Online Presence Beautiful: If a website is eye-catching, it will attract more visitors. Encourage the business that you are working with to team up with a graphic designer who can create cohesive logos and branding. This is an important, and often overlooked, step to owning a business. When things have a sense of cohesiveness, people feel more inclined to trust said business. This is also a reflection of the way the business chooses to stay organized.

- Email Lists: Getting people to sign up for a mailing list is a handy tool when it comes to marketing. When a business is able to stay in touch with their clients, they have a bigger chance of making a recurring sale. The mailing list can be a way for customers to receive exclusive deals or obtain early access to certain products. Encourage the business to stay on top of their list, sending out correspondence on a regular basis.

- Offer Free Samples: If it makes sense, sending out free samples of products could entice customers to make purchases. This is also a great way to convince people to sign up for a mailing list. People will not want to turn down a free product, so this can be a great way to quickly and effectively generate client outreach.

Why Ecommerce is a Successful Industry

When you seek a secondary income, it is important that you select an industry that is on the rise. This means, you want to choose a job that will be useful and in demand. Ecommerce has been a successful industry for quite some time now. Ever since the internet advanced in such ways that consumers were easily able to make purchases, the ecommerce marketplace saw major spikes in activity.

Not to mention, having a side income also means that you will probably have only a little bit of time to devote to this additional job. Ecommerce is all run online, and this is perfect for someone who already has plenty of in-person responsibilities. Consider how often you utilize the internet in your daily life -- this is why a job in ecommerce can become a successful source for you to make money.

The hardest part about this job is getting noticed by businesses and gaining their trust. It does take skill and creativity in order to figure out how to get the response that you are looking for, but with enough practice, it becomes easy. Much like other jobs, you need to ensure that you are creating a real connection with your potential clients. Treat every interaction with the same level of professionalism that you would expect to receive. This industry has a "snowball" effect; once you are in contact with the right people, the work falls into your lap.

Technology is not something that shows any signs of slowing down any time soon. As a society, we become more and more dependent on it as the years go on. You will be able to secure a future with a job in ecommerce, because it has proven to be useful for such a long stretch of time. As long as you are willing to put in the effort, you can reach any level of success that you desire.

Pros and Cons

Ecommerce isn't a new industry -- in fact, it has been popular for several decades now. Helping other businesses thrive can in turn become a great business for you to make extra money on the side. The task isn't as complicated as it seems. If you are willing to do some hands-on research, you can make a successful additional career for yourself from the comfort of your own computer.

Pros:

- You Have a Potential for Growth: You can begin by working for a single business, and eventually, you can take on more clients. Being an ecommerce agent gives you the ability to decide on your own level of work. If you need more to do, take on more clients! This freedom and potential are available to you from the very beginning.

- You Will Be a Part of a Top Industry: Getting a leading industry job can be difficult in most cases, but with ecommerce, you can get started with minimal experience. Unlike many other positions in ecommerce, you won't need a degree to work as an ecommerce agent. This means that you can choose to become a part of the industry at any given moment that you decide you want to start earning more money.

- Meeting New People Is a Perk: By approaching different businesses that you would like to work with, you will be building up your online social network. This is a way for you to meet a lot of new people in a short amount of time. Expanding your circle is beneficial both in a professional setting and a personal one. You might connect with businesses that you normally would not have, all thanks to your outreach.

- The Money Can Multiply: Once you get the hang of what it takes to be an ecommerce agent, you might find yourself available to take on more work. Remember, the more clients you have, the more money that you will be able to secure. As long as you are able to deliver your promised services, you will see successful results.

- You Get to Communicate With Others Frequently: If you consider yourself a people person, then ecommerce is a great side job to choose. One of the main tasks that you will have to do is communicate with others. Creating meaningful and honest connections with people is what makes for a good ecommerce agent. People can see past lies and gimmicks, even on the internet. If you can persuade customers to purchase products in an honest way, then you know that your skills are top notch.

Cons:

- There Is a Lot of Competition: Much like yourself, plenty of other people have probably seen what a great opportunity working in ecommerce can be. You will need to find ways to set yourself apart from the rest. Think about what makes you unique and what special skills you have to offer. Don't get discouraged if you do not get a job right away. Remember, one in every 10 people normally say yes.

- Pressure Is a Part of the Job: You are going to be expected to meet goals. Namely, you are going to be expected to generate sales for the business that you are working with. If this is something that you do not think you can handle or accomplish, then the ecommerce industry isn't the right industry for you. Being able to go with the flow is essential for working in a job like this.

- Getting Started Is the Hardest Part: You are going to need to do some preparation before you are able to serve businesses. Having knowledge about running an ecommerce store is one factor. The other is being able to approach businesses and convince them to hire you. The ease of these steps depends on if you are starting your own agency or working for an existing agency. Working for an existing agency might provide you with more training resources.

- Contracts Can End After Time: When you start working for a business, you might generate so much success for them that they will no longer see a need for your services. This is okay; it happens! The goal is to always have clients lined up to work with. When you become too comfortable in what you are currently doing, you might end up at a dead end. Being proactive about your work is the key to staying relevant in the industry.

- You Might Not Know How Much You Deserve: As discussed, it can be hard to give someone a price for your services, especially when you are new to the industry. You must work on your confidence when you are discussing budgets with your clients. Stand firm in your pricing, and those who are serious about working with you will make themselves known. You have to know that your pricing is a direct correlation to your skill set, and it is not wrong to want to be well compensated. This is what makes being an ecommerce agent an online side hustle.

Freelance Copywriting

Do you have a knack for selling with words? Utilizing your skills as a freelance copywriter could be a great potential source of additional income! No matter what the topic is, writers often seek outside help when it comes to making sure that their work is up to the correct standards. By working as a freelancer, you will have the opportunity to help writers on your own time. You will get to choose what jobs sound interesting to you and when you would like to work on them. This flexibility is what makes freelance copywriting one of the most popular side hustles that you can succeed in.

Freedom of Choice

Being a freelancer is one of the most flexible careers that you can choose. Normally, there are aspects of your day job that you most likely don't care to do. With freelancing, you get to pick which projects sound most interesting to you. There are several different deciding factors when it comes to taking on freelancing projects. If you are utilizing a website to find jobs, you will likely be able to use certain criteria to narrow down your search. Before you apply for these jobs, think about what interests you the most.

Once you have an idea of the topics you'd be willing to write about or edit, you can make customized searches. When you are trying to make an additional income, you have way more freedom of choice. This money is like bonus money, and that's the best part about it -- you have the ability to be selective. By only writing about topics that interest you, it is likely that the quality of your work will be much better than if you were writing about randomly assigned topics.

Alternatively, being a freelancer also means that you can be open to a wider range of tasks. It is truly up to your own personal preference. If you don't mind what you are going to be writing about, keep those search parameters open. Because you will continuously get different jobs, the work assigned to you will vary. Keeping your job interesting will encourage your creativity to flow.

Other than choosing which topics you want to write about, you also have the freedom to take on or pass up a job offer based on the employer. Applying for a freelancing job opens the lines of communication for both parties involved. You will get the chance to interview the employer in the same way that you get interviewed. Remember, this is not your full-time job. You should only work with those who you see true potential in. Don't feel bad for passing up offers that seem like more trouble than they are worth. Most freelancing jobs are temporary, so make sure that you are using your time wisely.

Negotiating Payments

At a traditional job, you are normally paid by the hour or with a salary. These norms are entirely different when it comes to freelancing. Generally, you will get paid per job when you freelance. This happens because you will likely work for several different people in a short period of time. Along with your freedom of choice when it comes to the jobs that you choose, you also get to have flexibility with the amount of money you earn.

When you are starting a freelance copywriting job, there will be an initial conversation with the employer. You will normally discuss the topic at hand and what the employer expects you to deliver. If you both feel that you meet all of the requirements, then you get to talk about price points. They will likely have an amount in mind, and you have the right to make suggestions on it. If you feel that the work is worth more than the amount being offered, ask for more money!

Think about your work as a freelancer as something that you don't need, but instead, something that you are actively choosing. You have the right to redefine your worth, and if the employer is not willing to pay you what you are asking, then you can politely decline the job. Many freelancers are scared to ask for what they actually think they deserve, but it just takes some practice. After some time, you will notice that your employers will respect you more if you are standing up for what you believe is fair.

Suggesting a price point is also a good way to weed out employers that are going to give you trouble. For example, if someone would like you to assist with copywriting a long novel for only $10, you will likely be over-exerting yourself for very little profit. Suggest that the budget be changed, and if the answer is no, you can move on to the next project. By establishing this boundary from the start of your career, you won't waste your time on draining projects that underpay.

Another example of a job that is troublesome is when the employer nitpicks your work without offering helpful suggestions. If someone is only going to pick apart what you worked hard on, with no clear conclusion in sight, this might be a job that you are going to want to pass up. Know that your time and efforts are just as valuable as anyone else's. This job is meant to supply you with additional income, and it shouldn't be causing you extreme amounts of stress or pressure.

If you don't know where to begin on fair pricing, think about an hourly rate that you think is fair. Also, you might want to consider what rate you think is fair per 100 words. With these two things in mind, you will be able to determine if the employer falls within your "fair pricing" range. All of this is a matter of opinion, but if you take a look at what some other freelancers normally charge, you might be able to gather some ideas for your own work.

Third-Party Websites

Anyone can be a freelance copywriter, but it is helpful to utilize online resources in order to put yourself ahead. The following are some ways you can give yourself a platform on which to get noticed as a freelancer:

- Upwork: This site is a hub for freelancers to connect with employers. You are able to sign up for a free account, get verified, and get started with working immediately after that. While Upwork is filled with all kinds of work, you are able to search for jobs that are a fit for your skills. So, if you excel in writing and editing, you can put this in your profile. By browsing through various job postings, you can get an idea of what work is available. This changes regularly, so make sure that you are checking Upwork frequently. Once you see some jobs that appeal to you, send a proposal. This is as simple as clicking a button -- You get to say a few words to the employer, and you can attach some writing samples if you have any. If the employer sees potential, they will set up an interview. It is during this process that you get to talk about the scope of the work and the amount that will be paid. Just as simple as this, you could get hired to work on the job. Sometimes, once the contract is over, the employer will end it. Other times, it can remain open and active, in case more work comes up in the future from that same employer. There is a lot you can do on Upwork, and as a freelancer, it can help your career flourish.

Pro-tip: Initially there looks like a lot of competition on Upwork. But if you niche down, you can easily charge high prices off the bat. For example, there are thousands of profiles listed as "copywriter", yet less than 10 with "Amazon copywriter" or "ClickFunnels Landing Page Copywriter"

- Monster: This is a general website for getting hired. You are able to create a profile and browse through thousands of job listings in your area. While it is not specifically tailored to freelancing, using Monster is a great way to expand your professional network. Because it has been around for such a long time, it is very well known. You will be able to search through freelance jobs, and apply for the ones that interest you most. A level of trust already exists between employers and future employees, because the platform is already well established. It is most likely that you are going to only find credible jobs that are posted on Monster, and this is important when you will be searching the listings frequently.

- Your Personal Website: Another approach to freelancing is to represent yourself. Creating your own website and promoting your skills is possible and a valid way to obtain jobs. Because you will be creating your own content, you will get to decide how you are represented. You can share as little or as much information about yourself as you'd like. As long as you are good with frequently checking your emails, running your own website to find jobs should not be an issue. While the customization features are a plus, remember that you might not get noticed as easily or as quickly when you are trying to freelance solo.

- There are several other websites that you can utilize as you search for jobs as a freelance copywriter. The best part is, you don't necessarily have to stick with just one! You can create your own website while still browsing through sites like Upwork and Monster. The more representation you have, the better your chances will be of earning jobs. With freelancing, the success that you see is very much dependent on the amount of work that you are willing to put in. Not only do you have to deliver as a copywriter, but you also need to become an expert at selling yourself. When you work in freelancing, you are the product that is being advertised. The skills that you have to offer will help clients to decide if they would like to work with you.

Gain Entrepreneur Skills

Being a freelance copywriter means that you will be wearing a lot of hats. You will have to come up with an idea of how to present yourself to others while highlighting your best skills. Then, you will have to live up to this promise and deliver the work discussed. The process continues and repeats for as long as you are willing to commit to it. This is one of the quickest ways to gain experience as an entrepreneur. Working for yourself is a great experience that can teach you a lot. All of the decision-making will be in your hands, and you will get to see the direct results of the choices that you make.

Once you get into the habit of representing yourself, this could lead to bigger opportunities in the future. Being a freelancer shows that you have the self-discipline necessary to get the work done because you want to, not because you have someone overseeing your actions. It provides you with a way to display your independence proudly, while also getting paid to do so! This is a positive experience, and many freelancers agree that they love the freedom that comes with the job.

Sometimes, it can be hard to stay motivated when it comes to working. Try easing into your workload to start. This way, you won't become overwhelmed. The great thing about choosing your own projects is that there are no limits; there is no such thing as not doing enough work. Earning a secondary income should feel this way! Once you feel that you have a grasp on the work, apply for some more jobs. Being a freelancer involves some trial and error, but only you will know what works best for your own schedule. Consider what other obligations you have, and only apply for jobs that you know will fit around them.

You will find that your organizational skills are going to come in handy as you start applying for these freelance copywriting jobs. Not only will you need to have the time to interact with your potential employers, but you will also need to make sure that you can get the work done in the allotted time. This is also something can can be negotiated between yourself and your employer. If you don't think that the given deadline is realistic, propose a new one! Being able to completely organize your workload will give you a great sense of control over the situation. You will know what is happening and when it is happening.

How to Build Your Reputation

When you are first starting out in a new field, one of the toughest parts can be establishing your reputation. Being a freelancer means working on your own time and finding your own projects. This also means that it is up to you to make clients take you seriously. This can seem like a difficult task, especially when you don't have a college degree on the topic. This is okay, though! Even newbies are able to find success by working as freelance copywriters. In order to gain experience, you must put in the work. Take jobs that vary from different topics and different clients.

By adding some variety to your list of work completed, you will be able to show future clients what you are capable of. A lot of employers will ask you for writing samples. This doesn't always need to be published work. If you have ever written any kind of essay before, you might be able to utilize it as a writing sample. Most employers just want to ensure that you are able to clearly piece together your sentences, and they want to know that you have great attention to detail. If you don't have anything written yet, picking a topic and writing 500 words on it could be helpful to add to your portfolio.

No matter what you are writing about, those who are looking at the quality of your work will be able to see a real example. This is how you boost trust with your clients. Eventually, as you work on more jobs, you will have more writing samples to provide to other employers. Many people are under the misconception that you cannot be a freelance copywriter unless you went to school for it. Nowadays, that isn't the case. Clients will hire you if you can present yourself in a trustworthy manner and if you can prove your skills.

Ask clients to leave you reviews and testimonials. On third-party websites, there is usually the option for both the client and yourself to review one another. This is a chance to express how it was to work with one another. Having other people vouch for you is a great indication of your skills and professionalism. If you are running your own website, including these testimonials on your site is a way to entice others to work with you, too. It can be nerve-wracking to ask for constructive criticism, but in the end, this is what will help you with building your reputation.

Writing For Blogs

When you are searching for work as a freelancer, consider approaching different blogs that you would like to be featured on. Plenty of blogs require outside help with writing and editing, so if you have any that you would like to work with, reach out! You will have nothing to lose by reaching out to someone who you want to collaborate with. The worst thing that can happen is they will say no, and then you can just move on and focus on the next task.

By copywriting for blogs that are already well established, you are furthering your career as a freelancer. This is a way for you to get your name out there to an audience that is guaranteed. If the readers respond well to your posts, you might be able to secure a regular job. Being a freelancer does involve a bit of risk-taking, but in the end, it can lead you to some pretty great opportunities. A lot of freelancers partner with blogs in order to gain momentum in their careers. If you aren't sure about joining a third party job site, starting by reaching out to some of your favorite blogs can be another way to enter the industry.

This is another way for you to work on a project-by-project basis. Writing for a blog normally does not involve any contracts to sign, so you will be able to keep your freedom. There are plenty of niches to choose from when it comes to blogs, so a little bit of brainstorming might be required on your end. Think about what you would most enjoy writing about. Do you like to inform people? Help people? Entertain people? The options are nearly endless.

Pros and Cons

When you have a keen eye, it just makes sense to put those skills to use. Freelance copywriters are in high demand for a lot of different projects. This can be quick side work for you to complete when you need some extra money to fill in the gaps. The more effort that you put into freelancing, the better results you will see.

Pros:

- Zero money needed to start: All you need is an internet connection. Even if you have no experience, you can start by reading copywriting blogs and advice on http://thegaryhalbertletter.com (Gary was considered the best copywriter alive for over 2 decades, and he has hundreds of articles available for free on his website). Another useful resource is Ben Settle's email list at http://bensettle.com

- Take on Work When You Need It: As a freelance copywriter, you get to decide if you'd like to work or not. Because the jobs are normally on a temporary basis, you can take on a couple of jobs when you'd like to have a little bit of extra money. If you are too busy to work more jobs, you don't need to apply for more. The system is pretty black and white; it works for a lot of people because of this reason.

- You Can Be Selective: Being picky is encouraged when you are doing any type of freelance work. Because the work does not last for a long period of time, you will need to make sure that you truly get along with the client. Make sure that you both understand the same vision and agree on the same price point. Being selective helps to ensure that your job as a freelancer is enjoyable.

- You'll Learn New Things: It is inevitable that you will be writing about topics you do not know much about yet. This is when your job also becomes a learning opportunity. By working on a piece of writing, you might have to do some personal research, and this can lead to some new information that you never would have looked into. Freelance copywriters see a wide variety of topics throughout their careers, and it might prove to be exciting.

- Traveling Isn't Required to Succeed: When you are doing freelance copywriting work, there is no need to even leave your house. Simply get on your computer and do what you need to do in the moment. Having a side job like this is great for those who are already feeling burnt out about their daily commute. You won't have to worry about being anywhere at a certain time. You'll only be responsible for the tasks that you choose to take on.

- Your Potential Is Unlimited: If you want to put a lot of time and effort into freelancing, you can. The amount of money that you earn is solely based on the ability that you put into the work. This is great for those who are looking for a way to earn money on the spot. If you are struggling with money for a few months, you can choose to take on some freelancing work. When you are okay financially, you will be able to ease up on your workload.

Cons:

- Getting Clients Can Be Challenging: It can be tough to

get your momentum going with freelance copywriting. If you have never done the work before, you will likely not have any contacts to approach. You need to be bold and risk-taking if you want to succeed in this job. Reaching out to people is one of the very first things that you will need to do to get hired.

- You Will Be Turned Down: Learning how to accept no for an answer is something that you are going to have to get used to. As a freelancer, you aren't always going to get picked for the job. There are a wide variety of reasons for this, but you will need to let it go. Don't take your declinations personally. Instead, utilize them as motivation to apply for something else.

- Clients Might Get Difficult to Work With: Because you are going to be working with so many people at any given time, you might experience some personality clashes. In case you don't see eye-to-eye with your client, you need to be able to effectively express this. Creative differences can and do pop up, and this is normal.

- The Work Can Be Inconsistent: You might experience periods of time when you have an abundance of work to choose from. On the other hand, you will also experience times when the work is lacking. This is something to keep in mind when you get into freelance copywriting -- inconsistency can happen, but this is something you should know about from the beginning.

- No One Will Work For You if You Cannot: Working on your own terms offers many levels of freedom, but if you are experiencing an illness or emergency, remember that nobody else will be able to fill in for you. The same applies for times that you are feeling overwhelmed with anything else going on in your life. Just be sure to only take on what you comfortably can before you overwork yourself.

Create Success on the Side

Many people opt to have a side hustle in order to keep their finances on track, and with all of the different jobs that can be completed solely online, it is easy to see why. From ecommerce to freelancing, you can secure a job that will work around your life and around your existing schedule. Earning an additional income does involve effort, but it doesn't have to be a stressful experience. The goal is to make your life easier, not harder than it needs to be. With the financial gain, you will be even more motivated than ever to work on these simple tasks online.

Remember, you don't necessarily need another degree or training in order to work online. The main aspect that is required is self-discipline. If you are able to navigate through tasks and keep yourself in check, you will find success with any additional job that you decide to take on. A lot of people make the mistake of overloading themselves with two full-time jobs, but you don't need to! Having a side hustle means having something that doesn't need to be a main priority in your life.

You should be able to work your additional job when you decide that you need to earn an extra income, not when you are already drowning in tasks. This income might not even be a necessity, but rather, a security net for you to rely on when your main source of income is getting low. Having this extra way to obtain money is like having a bonus in your professional life. The best part is, you can do just about anything that you have a passion for. Businesses are always in need of extra help, so do some brainstorming to think about which industries you can see yourself being a part of.

Having an additional job means that you are able to multitask efficiently. By using these skills, you are also expanding your ability to learn new things at a quicker pace. This is important when you are approaching tasks on your own. You will also be thinking like an entrepreneur, deciding what steps must be taken in order to succeed. One day, your extra side hustle might have the opportunity to turn into something bigger. There is truly no downside, as long as you are willing to put in the effort that is required.

Take some time to think about what direction you can see your life going in; think about what excites you, interests you. This is a great way to get an idea of the type of online job that you should seek. The ideas presented in this guide were meant to teach you about some of your options. They are jobs that a lot of others have found great success in, but you are not limited to only these choices. Think about what job you can take on that would make you the happiest, and do some research while you plan your approach. Having the tenacity and the ability to keep trying will get you far in your career.

www.ingramcontent.com/pod-product-compliance
Lightning Source LLC
Chambersburg PA
CBHW072143170526
45158CB00004BA/1490